ivi green™

Printed in the Russian Federation

ISBN: 978-1-7378751-0-9

LIFE SKILLS 101:
EVERYTHING YOU NEED, BUT WON'T LEARN IN SCHOOL

A Visual Guide

Boulder

Table of Contents

Why should I read this book? 7

Chapter 1. Who am I?

It all begins with principles 10

What is happiness? 12

Does it matter
what I think of myself? 14

How do I find my calling? 16

How do I set a goal and achieve it? 18

How are habits formed
and how do they affect me? 20

Perseverance or talent? 22

What is willpower
and how do I develop it? 24

What's next? 26

Chapter 2. My tools

Why do people learn? 30

How can I manage my time
effectively? 32

How can I stop getting distracted? 34

Why do I need
critical thinking? 36

How do I come up with new ideas? 38

Does everyone need systematic thinking? ... 40

How to save money, or
what is a budget? 42

What's next? 44

Chapter 3. My feelings and I

What is emotional intelligence? ... 48

What emotions do I experience? ... 50

What should I do with my feelings? ... 52

I don't know how to handle failure ... 54

What's next? ... 56

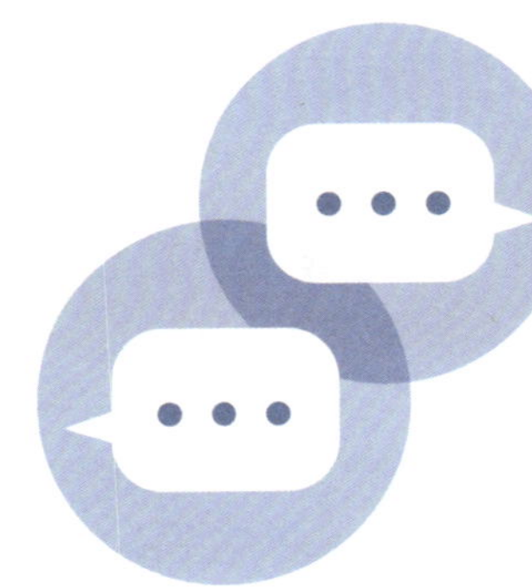

Chapter 4. Socializing

Should I tell the truth or not? ... 60

How can I truly listen? ... 62

Coming to an agreement ... 64

What if people judge me? ... 66

How should I share my ideas? ... 68

Public speaking ... 70

How can I write well? ... 72

What's next? ... 74

Chapter 5. Relationships

Why do I need friends? … 78

How do I work in a team? … 80

How do I understand my parents
and help them understand me? … 82

Dreaming of love … 84

What's next? … 86

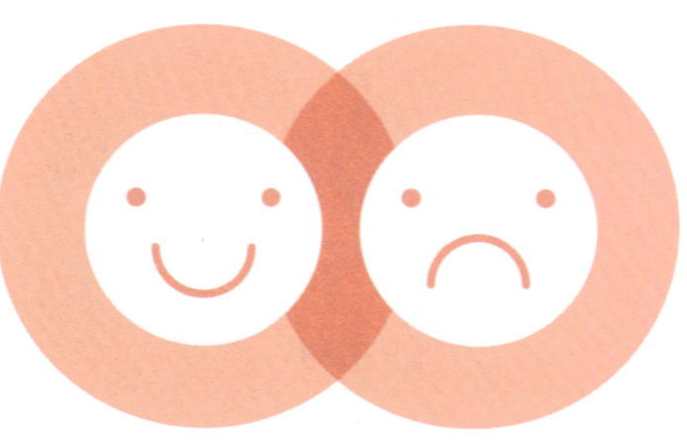

Chapter 6. My body and I

Why should I care about my health? … 90

How does my diet affect me? … 92

How do my gadgets affect me? … 94

Why are cigarettes,
alcohol and drugs bad for me? … 96

How does exercise affect me? … 98

What's next? … 100

References … 102

Why should I read this book?

Watch your actions, they become your habits.
Watch your habits, they become your character.
Watch your character, it becomes your destiny.

Your teenage years are an important and difficult time of your life. In the coming years, you will be making a variety of choices regarding school, career, health, friendships, love, relationships with others and with yourself. And much of what you learn and decide for yourself will affect your path in life farther down the line.

That's why it's important to start making decisions now about what you want to carry with you on your long journey, and what will only get in your way. What's more, you need to build good habits because what you do consistently gives you the most noticeable results.

When you answer the question, "Who am I?", you can then confidently choose in which direction you want to head.

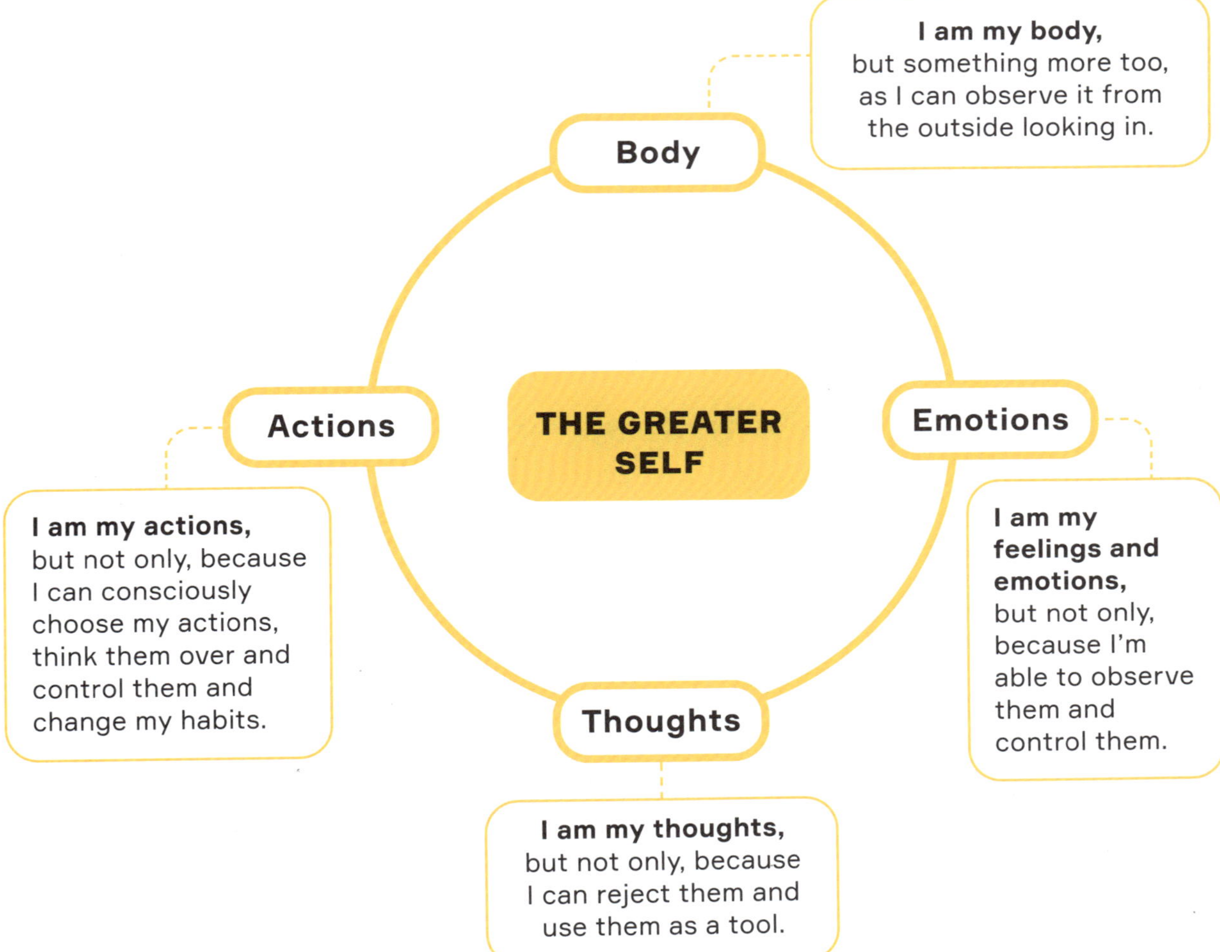

I am my body, emotions, thoughts and actions, plus something greater, something that allows me to be an observer, something that gives me support, something that helps me differentiate between good and bad. This is the part of me that chooses my life purpose.

CHAPTER 1

Who am I?

- **It all begins with principles**

- **What is happiness?**

- **Does it matter
  what I think of myself?**

- **How do I find my calling?**

- **How do I set a goal and achieve it?**

- **How are habits formed
  and how do they affect me?**

- **Perseverance or talent?**

- **What is willpower
  and how do I develop it?**

- **What's next?**

It all begins with principles

Principles are convictions about the world and yourself that reflect your core values. Your principles lie at the core of your actions and they greatly affect how you make choices in life.

The principles you live by will always be with you, even though they may change over time. They are the foundation on which you will build your life. It's those same principles that will help you overcome difficulties and remain balanced.

After you determine what your principles are, making important choices, even in the most tangled situations, will become easier.

Each person has principles. For example:

being kind　　**acting justly**　　**helping others**

How do I determine my own principles?

Regularly **remind yourself of actions** you've committed that make you proud.

Take notice of what occupies your thoughts and what you spend time on when you are not preoccupied with work.

Identify a bias you have against yourself (some negative trait you're known for or one you've convinced yourself exists) and do the opposite of what you ordinarily would do.

Think about what is most important in your life.

Throughout your day, try to **treat others the way you want to be treated.** How did you behave?

Listen closely to the words of your favorite songs. What is the artist trying to say? What in these words resonates in your heart?

When you find yourself in a difficult situation, think about what **someone you admire** would do and why?

Clean your "glasses"!

The "lens," or perspective, through which you see the world and your place in it, has to be meticulously cleaned. We often pick and choose facts that suit our point of view. For example, if you think that others don't wish you well, you will notice only expressions of ill will towards you. What you focus your attention on is what you get in return. Therefore, make an effort to look at the world objectively and try not think in stereotypes.

To strengthen your self-esteem, find a person who believes in you and learn to see yourself through his or her eyes. You will see the best in yourself, your unique characteristics and strengths. Focus on all the good that is inside of you.

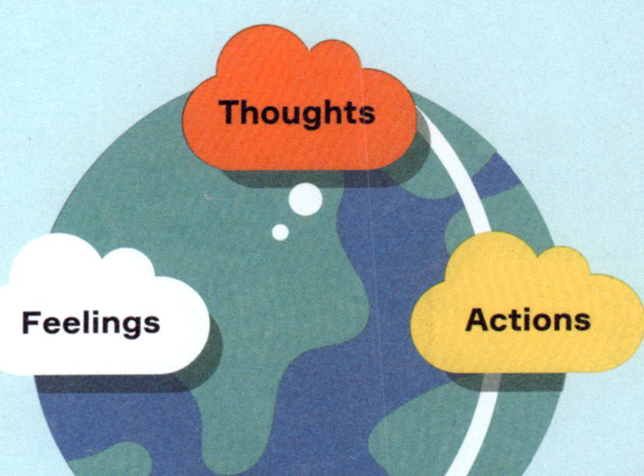

By virtue of your living amongst other people, your thoughts, feelings, and actions can have a colossal effect on them. It's up to you to decide what effect you will have on people and the world around you.

Your **principles, personal traits, and interests** are what make you unique. All together, they will manifest themselves in your actions.

You can express your individuality in various aspects of your life:

work

family

helping others

helping the planet

Why does the world need me?

Look around you. Everything that we use, everything that makes our lives easier and more interesting — safe cars, the Internet, a comfortable living space, consumer goods and much more — all this was, at some point, created by a person or a team of people.

And all these people were once children, contemplating their lives' paths. For some, that path is made clear early on by certain talents that become evident in childhood. And others spend their whole lives searching. **However, your path will twist and turn, so remember: you are completely unique, and there's no one out there quite like you!**

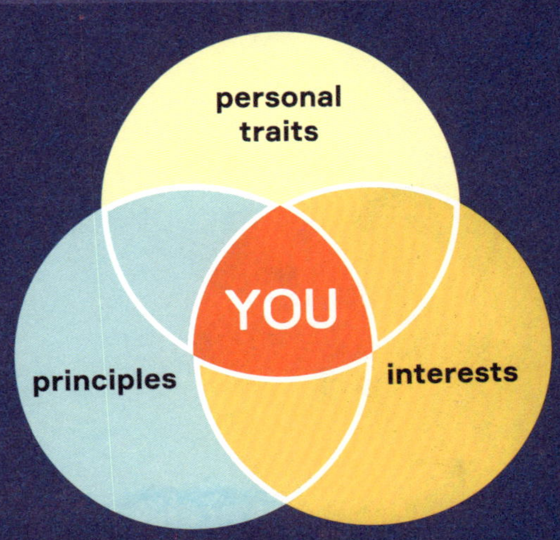

What is happiness?

According to a number of studies, happy people are more fortuitous and successful in their love, lives and friendships as well as in their work and careers. They also enjoy better health. But how do you become happy?

Happiness, contrary to how it is portrayed in advertising, isn't defined by external circumstances and surroundings. Happiness is an internal state.

Am I happy?

The only way to answer that question would be with a "yes" or a "no". Which would not be entirely correct. After all, happiness is neither some dot on a map, nor something that you can simply take possession of. Happiness is the journey. And your desire to keep moving forward and the joy you receive from advancing along that path are true signs of happiness.

Happiness is the route you choose in order to fully express yourself and the feeling of joy you experience as you travel it.

Can money buy happiness?

Psychologist David Myers says no. According to him, a person's level of happiness has very little to do with his or her income level, unless the person lives in extreme poverty. Frequently there can be an inverse relationship between the two: those who are well-off are in fact less happy and experience feelings of hopelessness and despair, and even after they have achieved their goals, they still aren't satisfied.

What does happiness mean to me?

1 Take a close look at **key parts** of your life: your school, your personal life, hobbies, social life, etc. What would you like to achieve in each one?

2 From the list that you come up with, choose the things that you **would most like** to achieve.

3 And now form a second list — things that you would **really, really like** to achieve.

4 Write down those innermost goals. Try to imagine **moving towards them**. In which scenario do you experience authentic engagement and enjoyment from the hard work you must do to get there? By following these four steps you are mapping your way to happiness.

The three sides to happiness

Happiness is in the discovery

Yes, this is possible, even though throughout your school years, you swore you could only feel happy during breaks. Learning new things and experimenting can immerse a person into the feeling of flow. That's the feeling of being completely "in the zone," when you are totally focused on a meaningful activity and during which you lose all sense of time because you're truly enjoying your work.

Happiness is in hard work

"Find a job you enjoy doing, and you will never have to work a day in your life." Working can feel like a slow and painful death, or it can be rewarding, especially if you are able to achieve self-realization in the process. In order to feel happy in your profession, search for your calling. Nobody said it was easy. Frequently people do what they're good at, not what they like doing, and those things aren't always one and the same. Ask yourself: What do I actually like doing? What type of activity brings me joy and gratification? To read further about purpose and the search for meaning, flip to p. 16.

Happiness is in your personal life

What sets happy people apart from others is the presence of deep, meaningful relationships in their lives. This is exactly why it's so important to carefully choose the people who surround you, and to know how to be a good friend and to love others. To read further about how to build healthy relationships, flip to pp. 78–85.

Does it matter what I think of myself?

What you think of yourself affects nearly every life choice you make. It's hard to be happy and build healthy, enduring relationships when you are not sure of yourself and constantly compare yourself to others. Valuing yourself is one of the most important skills a person can have.

What is self-esteem?

Self-esteem is how you measure your own worth and value.

People with high self-esteem will:
- confidently follow their own unique life-path
- set goals and achieve them
- feel secure and stable internally
- be able to handle difficulties and setbacks

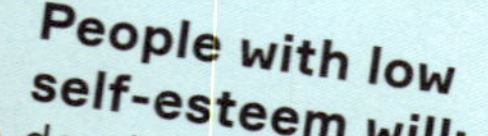

People with low self-esteem will:
- do what others expect of them
- reject and fear having responsibility for their own lives
- feel useless and unfulfilled
- be unable to thrive within their areas of interest or realize their talents

What's the difference between knowing your worth and being overly cocky?

People often confuse these two traits and mistake a person with high self-esteem for a person who thinks he or she is better than others.

In fact, **overly cocky people** inherently have low self-esteem, which they end up compensating for by acting superior or bringing down others.

At the same time, **being confident** means having respect for yourself and others. This is derived from being proud of and satisfied by your own accomplishments, regardless of what anybody else may think of you.

Try keeping a log of your accomplishments. Every day, do your best to write down something you've done or experienced that highlights your strong suits. Maybe you held your tongue and didn't talk back at a classmate, or kept a friend's secret, or performed outstandingly well during practice. Next time you're starting to get down on yourself, look back on this list and remind yourself of all the good things you've done and qualities you've exhibited.

Why do we criticize and underestimate ourselves?

 **Negative filter**

We tend to cling to negative events and replay them again and again in our heads, meanwhile, the good things in life often pass us by. When you notice yourself obsessing over something going wrong, ask yourself, "What's going right in my life? What is working? What am I fortunate to have?"

 **Personal defeats**

Embarrassing moments and failures work to solidify our negative self-perceptions. But if you learn to view downfalls as opportunities to learn and grow, moving forward with your life will become much easier.

 **Other people's perceptions**

There will always be those who will criticize and judge you. Don't take their words to heart. Let it be like water off a duck's back. You alone are responsible for your actions and not for people's reaction to them.

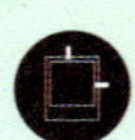 **Constant comparison**

Try not to compare yourself to others: each person has an individual path to walk and definition of happiness. By aiming to please others and measure up to their expectations, you stop living your life. It's better to compare the person you are today to the one you were yesterday. In what ways have you changed for the better? What have you worked on within yourself and achieved since then?

 **Guilt and shame**

Guilt, shame and self-criticism destroy one's self-esteem from within. If you feel guilt or shame for something you did, talk to the person you hurt, ask for forgiveness and forgive yourself.

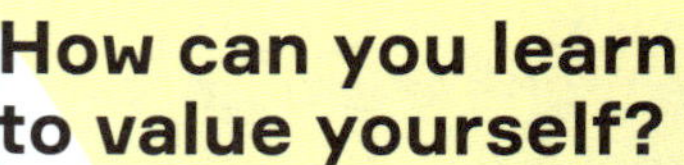

How can you learn to value yourself?

 **Know yourself**

What are you feeling? What do you really want out of life? What are your needs? Ask yourself these questions openly, honestly and without bias.

 **Accept responsibility for your own life**

Try making your next big life decision by yourself. Be guided by your own wants and needs, rather than what others may want for you. Weigh the pros and cons, ask your loved ones for advice, but make your own choice. Whatever the outcome may be, you will come out of this experience with more self-trust and feeling much stronger and more confident.

 **March to the beat of your own drum**

What are your values? What's important to you? What keeps you going? What makes life worth living? You are not obliged to live according to anyone else's expectations or fulfill someone else's dreams. Your life belongs to you and only you, and you get to choose how you want to live it.

 **Believe in yourself**

Remember that you are unique. There is no one out there like you. Therefore, you deserve happiness as much as the next person does.

How do I find my calling?

Each of us has something that he or she loves to do. Some people love playing the drums, others love staring up at the night sky. Someone may be fascinated with film, while somebody else enjoys basketball. For a lucky few, the thing that they love doing becomes their career. We often say that those people have found their calling.

What does it mean to find your calling?

Your calling is something that allows you to reach your potential, while encompassing your interests and talents. Finding your calling fills your life with meaning.

The "Find-it" Formula

Your calling (a.k.a. your purpose) is the point where your interests, your desires, your abilities and your opportunities all meet.

Interests
What do you enjoy doing?

Opportunities
Is there an opportunity for you to do this?

PURPOSE

Desires
What would you want to do every day, given the chance?

Abilities
What can you do well?

You can tell you've found your calling when...

You're able to do what you love and love what you do

You feel at one with yourself and the world around you

You don't doubt yourself or the purpose of your being here on Earth

Do I have a calling?

Yes, because everyone has one, but not everyone knows right away what his or her calling is. A calling is meant to be discovered; the search for it might come easily for some, or take many years for others.

Moreover, your calling doesn't have to be just one thing. You can identify many different things as your calling. For example, someone might combine writing books with performing on stage — both activities being loved equally. Or, someone who's made a name for herself in programming can also coach football games at the local elementary school on weekends.

QUICK QUIZ
How to tell if you've already found your calling

Mark if you agree:

- [ ] a "thing" that brings you joy and satisfaction — so much so that you lose track of time while doing it

- [ ] you've been interested in it for a long time

- [ ] it's something you're able to do well

- [ ] when run into difficulties, you don't let that stop you and you keep working on it

- [ ] you're always raising the bar for yourself and continually improving

- [ ] when your friends and family talk about you, they can't help but bring up your interest in it

- [ ] you know like-minded people

- [ ] you can see yourself doing it for the rest of your life

? *How many did you cross off? The more of these you can relate to, the higher the chance that you're on the right track to discovering your calling.*

Exercises to help you find your calling

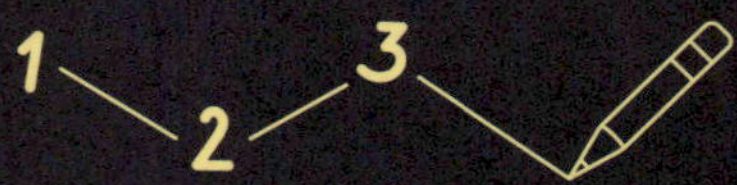

10 favorite activities
Write down 10 things you love doing, no matter how mundane or trivial they may seem. Which of these things might be it? Try to test them using the quiz to the left.

Outside perspective
Ask a friend or parents to describe your strong suits and write down everything they say. Too often we dismiss our own talents, which is why having an outside perspective might come in handy.

The perfect day
Describe your ideal day. What is it like? What would you do?

How do I set a goal and achieve it?

Everyone has dreams. Sometimes those dreams consist of simple things, and other times they are so ambitious that they seem unattainable. In any case, when you're able to put a dream into words clearly and specifically, that dream becomes a goal.

Dream: *I want to see the world*

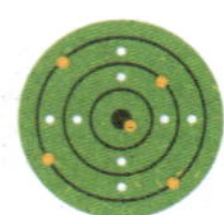

Goal: *By the time I'm 35, I will have been to every European country and lived in each one for two weeks*

How do I turn a dream into a goal?

For a dream to become a goal, you must boil it down to specific details and plan the steps you will take to get there.

Create a step-by-step plan
What steps will you need to take in order to achieve this goal? Write them out and try to break them down into bite-sized pieces.

How do I articulate my plan?

A famous method for this is called "setting **SMART** goals". In order for your goal to be considered a SMART goal, it must be:

 **S**pecific

 **M**easurable

 **A**chievable

 **R**elevant

 **T**ime-bound

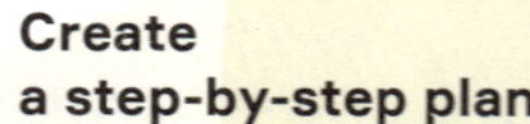

2

Come up with a SMART goal

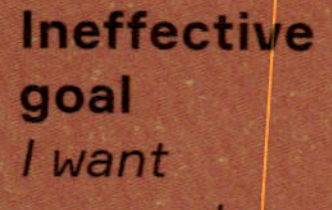
Ineffective goal
I want a new phone

SMART goal
To buy myself a new iPhone with my own money for my next birthday

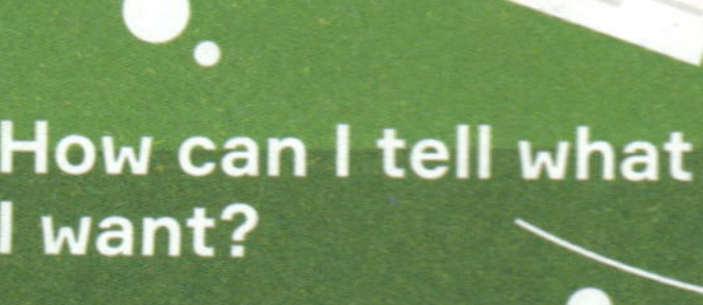

5

Celebrate!

When you finally get where you want to be, don't forget to celebrate! Acknowledging the results of your hard work will motivate you to take on your next personal quest and give you even more confidence.

4

Carry out your plan

A helpful exercise is to draw a timeline and color in every step you complete. This will allow you to track your progress visually, which will keep you motivated.

3

1

Choose a goal

This is where your list, journal and vision board will come in handy!

Is it possible to live without a goal?

A lot of people do, but, generally, they are less satisfied with their lives and feel lost as they lack a clear sense of direction. Try conducting an experiment: ask some people who you think have accomplished something how they got to where they are now. Most likely, they will tell you that they started out by setting a goal for themselves.

It's incredibly important to develop the habit of asking yourself what you really want. We have so many different responsibilities and expectations put on us that it's easy to lose sight of our own desires. What others want for us and what we want for ourselves can either coincide or cause us to stray from our true paths, making it more difficult to eventually get back on track.

What will help you achieve your goal?

Manage your time (flip to p. 32)

Tell people about it

Don't be afraid to ask for help

Envision how you will feel when cross the finish line

Make a list

For example, "What do I want to achieve by the time I'm 20." Remember, do not reject any ideas, no matter how wild, grand or generic they may be.

Make a vision board

A vision board is a collage of photos and pictures that reflect your ideal future. Don't forget to update it!

Start keeping a journal

Make it a habit to write down your dreams and thoughts about your ideas.

How are habits formed and how do they affect me?

A habit is something you do automatically, without thinking, like chewing on your pencils or compulsively checking your phone every five minutes. Alternatively, you can also make your bed and brush your teeth every morning by habit. Any action you complete "on autopilot" is a habitual action.

How are habits formed?

time

+

regular repetition

=

habit

For a habit to form, you need to do it over and over, consistently, for a long period of time. Your brain will remember your regular actions and start helping you perform them without needing much energy or effort.

Habits can affect us even when we don't want them to. For example, if your parents watch TV every night at dinner, and you all eat together, you're also going to get accustomed to that daily ritual.

Habits can also be based on personal choice. For instance, you can choose consciously to start walking up the stairs to the fifth story every day instead of waiting for the elevator.

Why do we need habits?

Habits save energy and effort in a very natural way. They make our lives easier. You do a lot of things automatically. Meanwhile, your brain can focus on more important things.

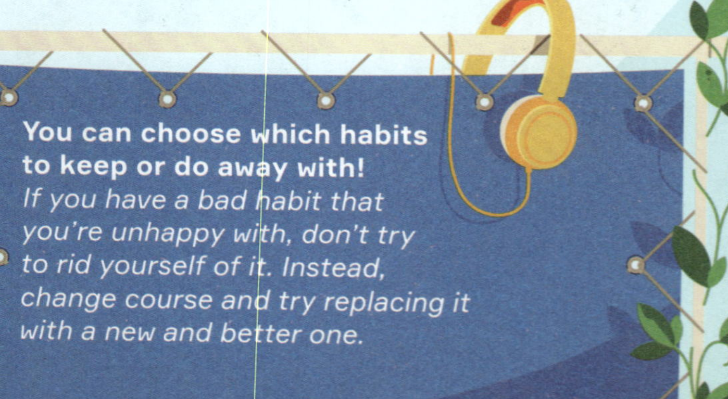

You can choose which habits to keep or do away with!
If you have a bad habit that you're unhappy with, don't try to rid yourself of it. Instead, change course and try replacing it with a new and better one.

Ok, habits make life easier. But how do they affect me?

When you do something out of habit, you often don't notice or pay attention to your actions. As it turns out, habits are the true rulers of your life. And hopefully we are talking about good habits.

Pay attention to your routines. Do you rely on any habits?

How do I form a new habit?

Choose what habit you want to build
Start small: if you decide to start a habit of reading in another language, don't start out by reading some lengthy, complicated book. Instead, read short articles about something you're interested in.

Ask yourself why this habit is good for you
Ask yourself this question several times to really get to the bottom of it. Understanding why you started in the first place will help you overcome laziness and wavering doubt.

Create a twenty-day plan and follow it
It is believed that it takes 20–30 days to form a persistent habit.

When you're done, get your reward!
Chances are by this time your habit will have become cemented in your brain. And once you receive the reward you promised yourself, the victory will be that much sweeter.

Reward yourself for your efforts
You can do this by giving yourself small rewards for every step of the way, or one big one for having made it to the end.

Say no to self-criticism!
It's no big deal if you miss a day or two. Save the energy you would've spent on beating yourself up (which never works anyway) and channel it towards understanding what went wrong and what you can do differently tomorrow.

Record your progress
Keep track of how you're doing. Write check marks in your planner, circle days in your calendar, use stickers — do it however feels best for you.

Help yourself — make the journey easier
Leave yourself little hints and stepping stones that will come in handy at the right moment. If your goal is to eat more fruit, wash them ahead of time and set them in a bowl on your dining table. If you want to run in the mornings, place your running shoes on your doormat.

Remember: your habits are entirely in your hands. You're the boss here!

Perseverance or talent?

You've probably heard how some revolutionary thinker was an average student, or how a famous athlete was not very good at sports in school. Not everything is determined by talent. Success is often the product of our perseverance.

And it is a whole lot easier to pursue your goal once you realize it has the potential to help others. Regardless of what you do, whether you're a programmer or a painter, or whether you are interested in languages or insects, there is always some way to apply your craft so that it can change people's lives for the better.

What is perseverance?

The ability to overcome difficulties and keep moving forward regardless of every bump along the way.

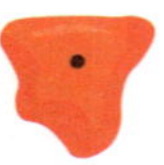

The ability to learn and constantly acquire new skills, which you can then master and perfect.

Why is it hard to persevere?

By design, it's not easy to show determination — you don't always have the emotional strength and willpower to force yourself to do something challenging.

If I have talent, why do I need perseverance?

Talent is simply an indicator of your potential, and it's your choice whether you reach your potential or not. Having perfect pitch and a great sense of rhythm won't make you a concert musician. The missing element in this equation is constant practice. Look at the success equation by Angela Duckworth.

Talent shows the speed with which you'll learn a certain skill if you apply yourself and put in the necessary effort.

If you want to become an expert at something you're naturally good at, you'll need to be doubly determined.

Find what truly engages you

If there isn't an activity or area that immediately stands out to you as being interesting, search for it deliberately. Listen to your heart and take note of what lifts your spirits and motivates you. Should you discover that you don't like some aspect of it, don't immediately quit; this may simply be a momentary setback. The longer you do something, the clearer it will be whether that activity is suited for you or not.

Don't lose interest

Remember, it's normal when your interest in an activity begins to fade or disappears altogether. In order to reignite that passion, ask yourself: what else is there to learn? Can I gain some additional knowledge from this activity?

Work on your weaknesses

Often we choose to ignore the metaphorical chinks in our armor. Working on our weaknesses in an area improves our overall performance, so don't be afraid to ask for and apply constructive criticism. Maybe you have a large vocabulary, but your sentence structure needs work — your English teacher may be able to help.

Help yourself

It will be easier to start taking lessons or training if you turn those activities into habits. To read more about how habits are created, flip to p. 20.

What will help me?

You'll be more likely to keep going and succeed if you have:

Believe in yourself

You're going to stumble. The best of the best and the most successful people still do. Fall seven times, get up eight; ask yourself what went wrong, dust yourself off and keep going.

Try to stay positive

If others doubt your abilities, don't take their skepticism to heart and don't allow them to change your mind. Instead, pause and ask yourself, "Is this really true? How else can I look at the situation? Can I take something positive out of it?"

Ask for help

It's really important to ask for and receive help from your close circle: parents, teachers, coaches and friends. They will help you tackle challenges and offer you the necessary support to keep you going.

What is willpower and how do I develop it?

Do you find yourself putting things off until later? Do you rarely finish what you started? Do you promise yourself you'll go for a morning run or study for an exam but never follow through? If you answered yes to these questions, you may be lacking in willpower.

Why do some have willpower, while others don't?

Actually, the truth is that everyone has willpower. It's just more developed in some than in others.

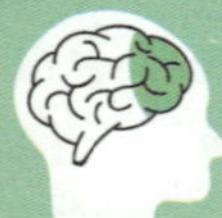

According to Kelly McGonigal willpower has to do with our brains. In the prefrontal cortex (which sits behind our forehead and eyes) there are three areas responsible for the following functions:

I will not
Helps us notice and respond appropriately to our impulses and urges, stopping us from acting rashly.

I want
Tracks our genuine wishes, helps us focus on completing tasks and rejects impulsive desires.

I will
Responsible for our long-term goals; aids us in completing boring, difficult tasks that don't show immediate results.

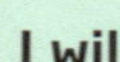

A person has willpower when he is able to regulate these three aspects:

I will
I will not
I want

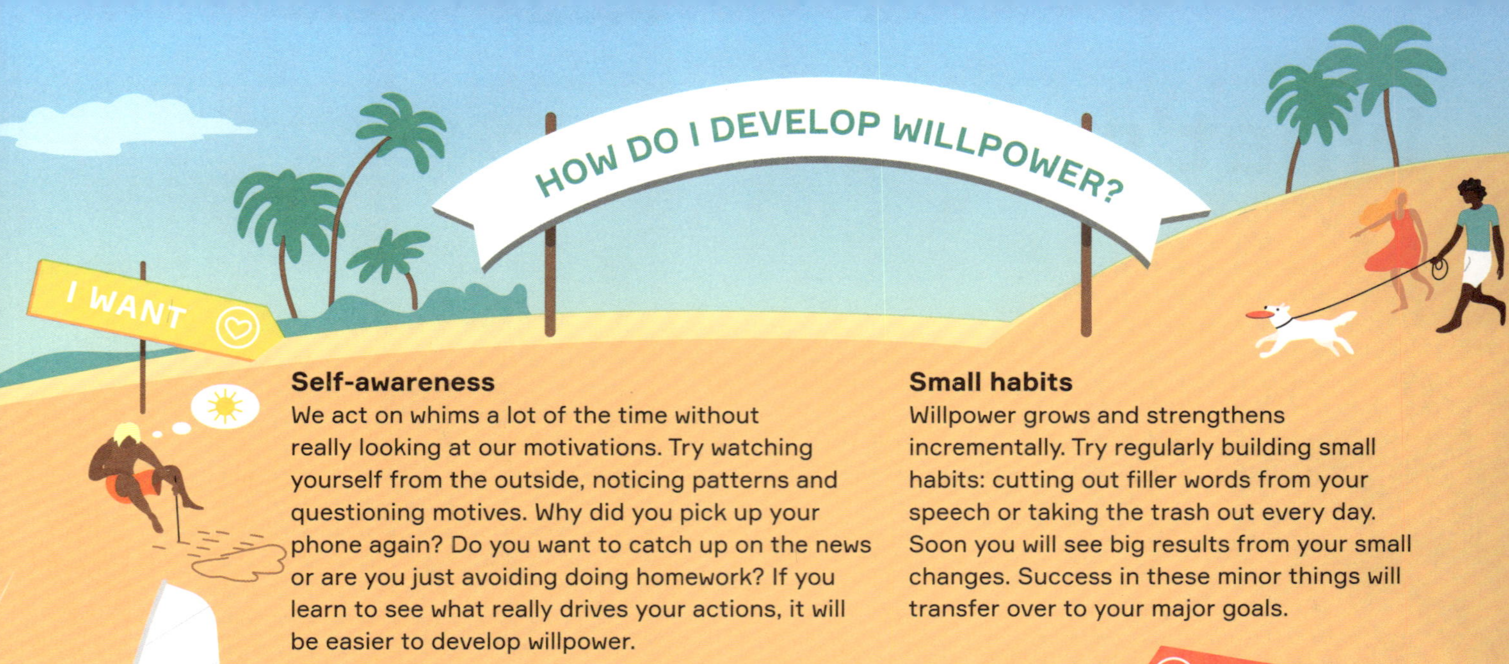

Self-awareness

We act on whims a lot of the time without really looking at our motivations. Try watching yourself from the outside, noticing patterns and questioning motives. Why did you pick up your phone again? Do you want to catch up on the news or are you just avoiding doing homework? If you learn to see what really drives your actions, it will be easier to develop willpower.

Small habits

Willpower grows and strengthens incrementally. Try regularly building small habits: cutting out filler words from your speech or taking the trash out every day. Soon you will see big results from your small changes. Success in these minor things will transfer over to your major goals.

Prioritizing

Focus on one thing. It's unrealistic to get better at chemistry, learn French, and read three books from your summer reading list all at once. But you can do these things one at a time, which will give you a better chance at succeeding.

The 10-minute rule

If you don't feel like doing something, just start and promise yourself that you can quit after ten minutes. Most likely, when the time is up, you'll have already got into the groove of things and won't want to stop.

Today and tomorrow are no different

Thinking about leaving something for tomorrow? Remember: tomorrow will come, and it will be just like today, with its own to-do list, so the thing that you want to put off will be just as inconvenient the next day. So what is the point of delaying it?

Concentration

Taking a minute to concentrate on your breathing or on the second hand on the clock develops your ability to concentrate and control your impulses.

What will help you along the way?

Our brain, like any muscle, gets fatigued, and needs energy to rejuvenate. When you don't have a lot of energy, the brain always chooses the easiest path: it gives in to temptations and ignores your long-term goals.

On the contrary, if you're full of energy, it will be a lot easier to demonstrate willpower. Help yourself develop willpower by paying attention to what energizes you, as well as what drains you.

It's difficult to use willpower when you: 
- are tired
- didn't sleep well
- are experiencing strong negative emotions

It will help if you:
- rest
- sleep
- exercise
- experience positive emotions
- celebrate your previous wins

What's next?

Think about:

These questions will help you understand yourself better. Come back to them once every couple of months.

- What do you love about yourself? What makes you unique? What sets you apart?
- What do you admire in other people? Why?
- When do you feel the happiest? What are you doing in those moments?
- What do you get praise for? What do others ask you for help with?
- What do you dream about? Do you have a plan of action? Do you know how to turn your dreams into goals?
- Who's in your support group? Who's going to help you along the way?

What to read:

- **What Do You Really Want? How to Set a Goal and Go for It!** by Beverly K. Bachel

- **Roadmap: The Get-It-Together Guide for Figuring Out What to Do with Your Life** by Brian McAllister, Mike Marriner and Nathan Gebhard

- **The Element: How Finding Your Passion Changes Everything** by Ken Robinson and Lou Aronica

Your tools:

- Vision board
- Journal/diary
- Habit tracker
- List of your wins

What to watch:

8 secrets of success
by Richard St. John

Grit: The power of passion and perseverance by
Angela Lee Duckworth

CHAPTER 2

My tools

- Why do people learn?

- How can I manage my time effectively?

- How do I stop getting distracted?

- Why do I need critical thinking?

- How do I come up with new ideas?

- Does everyone need systematic thinking?

- How to save money, or what is a budget?

- What's next?

Why do people learn?

Nowedays people learn over their entire lives. Even after getting a degree, we continue to gain new knowledge every day. As it continues to develop, your brain allows you to lead an interesting life, full of new ambitions.

Why do we have to keep learning?

The world is changing more rapidly than ever. New discoveries are being made and new technology is being invented at this very moment.

The average lifespan is increasing; now you can have several different careers and learn many trades throughout your life.

Continuous learning is good for your brain and ensures that you'll be able to think clearly irrespective of your age.

What is there to learn?

Learning isn't just about acquiring new information, like we do in school.

It goes hand-in-hand with the development of life skills. A person in modern times should be able to:

Solve difficult problems

Think critically

Come up with original ideas

Work in a team

Communicate

Manage his or her emotions

Make choices

These are exactly the types of skills this book will share with you. However, it won't be enough to simply read the book if you want to master them — you will need to buckle down and put them into practice. The good news is: it's okay to take things step by step.

What's going to help me learn?

Remember — your brain is flexible
Every time you learn a new skill or memorize a new fact, your brain creates so-called "neural pathways" that will make that task easier to do in the future. Your brain is easily moldable, like playdough, and it's constantly changing, so learning new things isn't as difficult as it sounds.

Learn slowly
A common misconception is that all intelligent people are quick learners. However, skills are solidified when you go in-depth into a subject, taking it slowly and steadily. How quickly you gain a skill has nothing to do with your intelligence.

Collaborate
Exchanging ideas and thinking collaboratively with others improves the quality of learning and helps build neural pathways more effectively. Discuss topics with your classmates, and don't be afraid to ask questions and ask for help.

Appreciate your mistakes
We learn more quickly and productively when we have to overcome barriers and correct mistakes. This is an integral part of learning.

Is it true that learning gets more and more difficult with age?

Scientists confirm that there are no limits to how much our brains can grow. Regardless of age, you can always master a new skill or learn something new. But, like any muscle, our brain has to be exercised so that it doesn't deteriorate, and this is where you come in.

How can I manage my time effectively?

People who have a good grasp of time management are more likely to achieve their goals by fitting more into their schedule while using less energy. Why? Because they make time for rest! What's their secret?

1 Put everything in one spot

Instead of spending energy on trying to memorize all that needs to be done, write all your tasks down in one spot, like a notebook or the notes app on your phone. This way, you won't have to worry about forgetting something.

2 Sort your tasks into lists

In your **calendar,** note tasks that need to be done at a specific date and time. For example, every Tuesday you have band practice, and next Wednesday you have a doctor's appointment. Write down upcoming events at the start of every week and update your calendar when something new comes up.

Larger tasks consisting of more than one step should be put under the **"projects" list.** This list might include your biology presentation: first, you have to choose a topic; then do your research; make the presentation itself; and, finally, present it to the class. This list will help you keep track of what projects are currently in the works and what needs to be done to complete them, so they don't get lost in your routine or daily tasks.

The famous **"to-do list"** itself is a complete list of everything that doesn't have a specific time restriction. It can hold the smaller steps that need to be taken to complete your projects, or small tasks, like helping your parents clean the house.

Your **"someday" list** consists of plans and dreams that you would like to fulfill at some point in your life. When you have the time and the circumstances are right, you'll remember what you have always wanted to do.

Look over your lists on a regular basis — at least once a week. Some tasks may lose their urgency and importance, while new ones might come up.

CALENDAR
October
Sun Mon Tue Wed Thu Fri Sat
1   2   3   4   5   6   7
     Music Dentist
     7:00 p.m. 2:00 p.m.
8   9   10   11   12   13   14
     Music
     7:00 p.m.
15   16   17   18   19   20   21
     Music   Lena's
     7:00 p.m.   birthday
22   23   24   25   26   27   28
     Music
     7:00 p.m.
29   30   31
     Music
     7:00 p.m.

You can learn how to set goals for yourself on p. 18

PROJECTS
Pass math final
Do bio presentation
Prepare for exchange trip to England

TO-DO LIST
✓ Math H/W
✓ English essay
✓ Choose topic for bio presentation
  Fill out questionnaire
✓ Read about program on website
  Organize closet
✓ Clean fish tank
  Choose gift for Lena
  Write a letter to host family

SOMEDAY
Film stop motion
Learn how to play the ukulele

3 Get things done
Before getting started, ask yourself:

Which task is the most important? Which one has to be completed as soon as possible?

Fill out questionnaire

What do you have time for this very moment? What can you get done right where you are with the tools at hand?

Read about program on website

How do you feel and what do you have enough energy for?

Write a letter to host family

Don't forget to unwind! Set periods of time throughout the day when you can cross things off your to-do list (like breaks between classes). It's also crucial to have off days when you aren't obligated to do anything from your lists and can focus on alleviating your stress.

How do I stop getting distracted?

Sometimes we ruin our own plans by letting ourselves get distracted; we find ourselves doing something completely unrelated and unproductive, even though we were trying to get things done. It's possible to overcome this. All you have to do is calm down your "monkey mind" and take back control.

The "monkey mind" part of the brain

Only chases after pleasure

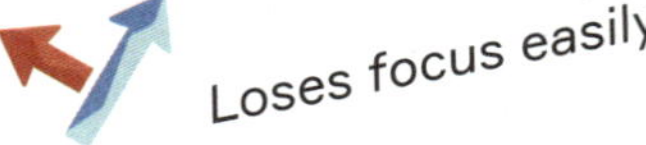
Has no sense of time

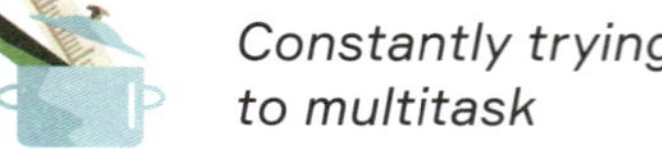
Loses focus easily

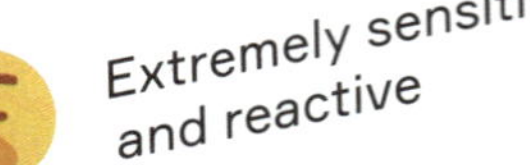
Constantly trying to multitask

Extremely sensitive and reactive

Clearing your memory

Your brain remembers and holds on to all your unfinished tasks. If you promised a friend that you'd lend her a book, you might forget about it during the day, but as soon as you're in bed and falling asleep — there it is! It will be hard to doze off, because your "monkey mind" demands that the task be done immediately. The lists we talked about on p. 32 will come in handy at times like these.

Let's say you were writing an essay when a friend started talking to you about his weekend plans. You allowed yourself to get sidetracked, and when you returned to your previous task, you couldn't pick up where you left off right away. It took you some time to get back into the groove.

Changing focus is energy-consuming!

It might seem like you can easily do several tasks at once: watch a TV show, do a school assignment, respond to text messages. But when you switch your focus from one thing to another, your brain has to spend more energy and make an extra effort, which ends up hurting rather than helping your productivity.

Pause

If you find your mind wandering, the first step to take is to pause and become aware of it. Observe the monkey and use your willpower to not give in to its whims.

Meditation

Works wonders for your ability to concentrate. Taking three full breaths while exhaling slowly after each will help you switch between tasks and focus on what you're doing.

Rest

Sometimes you really are at the brink of your capacity to focus and need a break. In that case, switch things up: if you have been reading, go take a walk or put on some music and dance. Put a time limit on how long your break will be and when the time is up, return to the unfinished task and plan ahead for when your next recess will be.

Plan

Sometimes you can't seem to focus because there's something else on your mind, like an upcoming audition or exam. In that case, make a plan of action. Making lists or creating roadmaps to the desired results will unburden your brain and help you feel more prepared.

Intervals

Try working in intervals: 20 minutes of hyper-focused, meticulous work, then 5–10 minutes of rest. This is the Pomodoro Technique, and there's an app specifically designed to help you employ it in a fun, game-like way.

Why do I need critical thinking?

We live in a world where we have direct access to any and all sources of information, so it's crucial that we develop skills to know what we can and cannot believe. We have to learn to discern important, fact-based knowledge from trivial speculation, and we can't do that if we don't use critical thinking.

To think critically is to:

1 Understand and evaluate judgements

- challenge arguments and ideas
- form logical thought processes
- compare thought processes
- be critical of thought processes

2 Understand and evaluate evidence

- search for reliable sources
- extract the important information
- confirm the validity of sources

3 Take into account the biases and/or filters of yourself and others

Do I know how to think critically?

Not thinking critically means blindly trusting anything you hear, looking for and finding proof only of your side of the argument, completely ignoring anything that disproves your beliefs.

What is critical thinking?

draw evidence-based conclusions and act in accordance with them

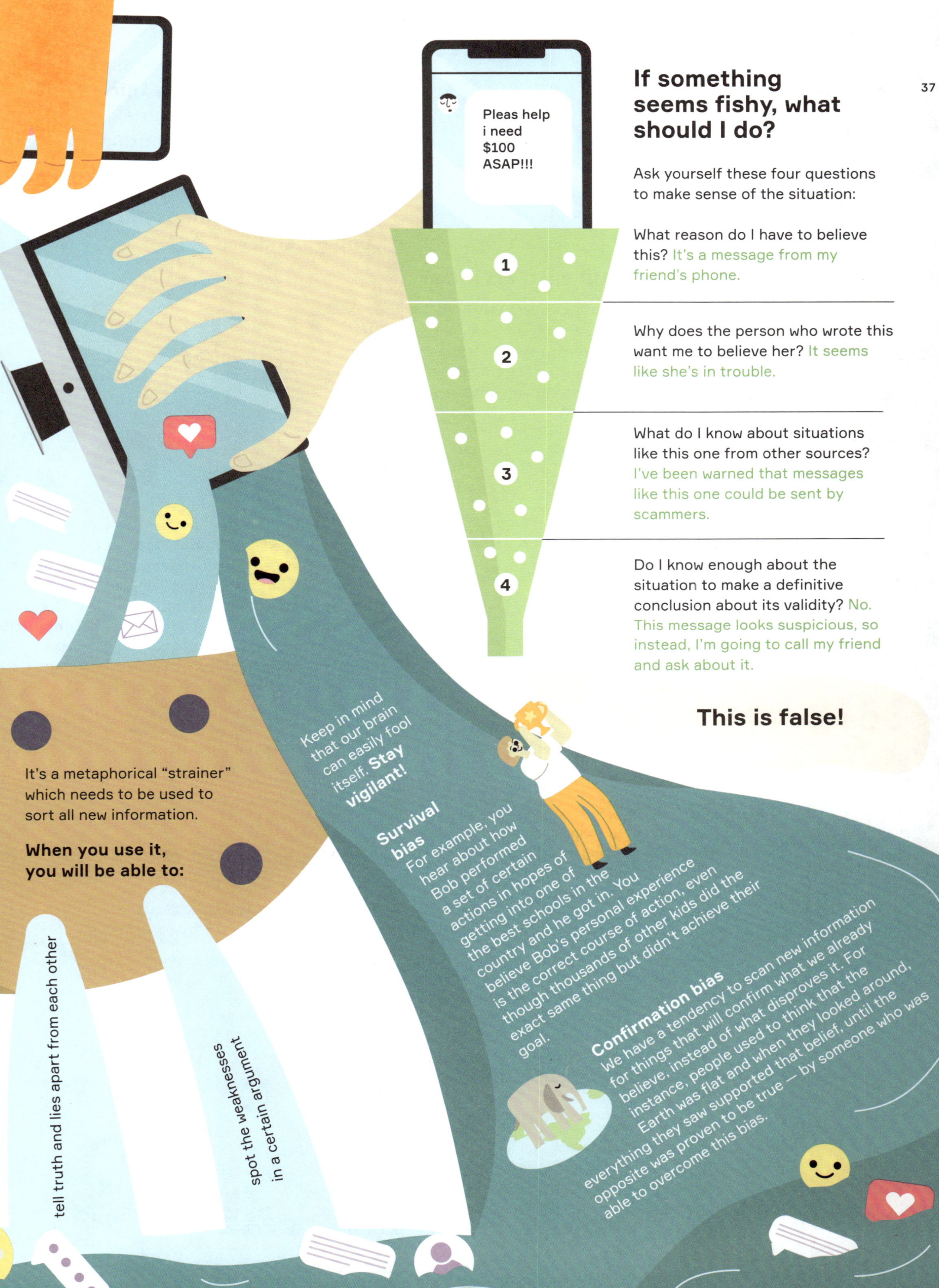

If something seems fishy, what should I do?

Ask yourself these four questions to make sense of the situation:

1 What reason do I have to believe this? It's a message from my friend's phone.

2 Why does the person who wrote this want me to believe her? It seems like she's in trouble.

3 What do I know about situations like this one from other sources? I've been warned that messages like this one could be sent by scammers.

4 Do I know enough about the situation to make a definitive conclusion about its validity? No. This message looks suspicious, so instead, I'm going to call my friend and ask about it.

This is false!

It's a metaphorical "strainer" which needs to be used to sort all new information.

When you use it, you will be able to:

tell truth and lies apart from each other

spot the weaknesses in a certain argument

Keep in mind that our brain can easily fool itself. **Stay vigilant!**

Survival bias
For example, you hear about how Bob performed a set of certain actions in hopes of getting into one of the best schools in the country and he got in. You believe Bob's personal experience is the correct course of action, even though thousands of other kids did the exact same thing but didn't achieve their goal.

Confirmation bias
We have a tendency to scan new information for things that will confirm what we already believe, instead of what disproves it. For instance, people used to think that the Earth was flat and when they looked around, everything they saw supported that belief, until the opposite was proven to be true — by someone who was able to overcome this bias.

How do I come up with new ideas?

Creativity is a priceless skill in modern day life. Many things can be and are done by machines, but how to think in an unconventional way and find unique, new solutions isn't something they know how to do just yet. That's where you have the upper hand.

How do I come up with an idea?

You can picture the thoughts you think day in and day out as a highway, from which there are different exit ramps, which we generally speed right past without even noticing them. But if you allow your thoughts to take a different, unexpected turn, you might just come up with something original and new.

Methods for sparking your creativity

These simple exercises will help you "take the next exit" — look at ordinary things in a fresh light and come up with truly creative solutions to everyday problems.

Come up with as much as you can

If you need an **original idea,** like what you're going to get for your friend's birthday, try this method: come up with fifty ideas in thirty minutes. Let your mind run free and don't reject any of your thoughts; don't filter the ideas quite yet. Write down everything that comes to mind. After you're done, read over your list and pick the best one. You can use the Six Thinking Hats method for this.

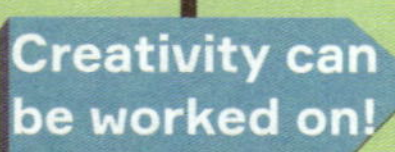

Every day for two weeks, come up with **five new ways** of using an ordinary, run-of-the-mill object. What can a pan be used for? What about a cutting board? Pick a new item every day.

If you get stuck and your mind goes blank, try adding a completely **random word** to whatever you're focusing on. For example, "gift" and "battery"— maybe this word association will give birth to the idea of gifting your friend a heated blanket.

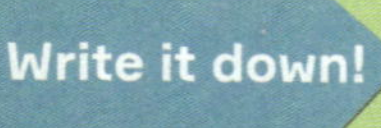

Ideas get lost. Get a notebook where you can record any and all ideas that pop into your head. **Look through it occasionally;** maybe the time has come to realize a few of them.

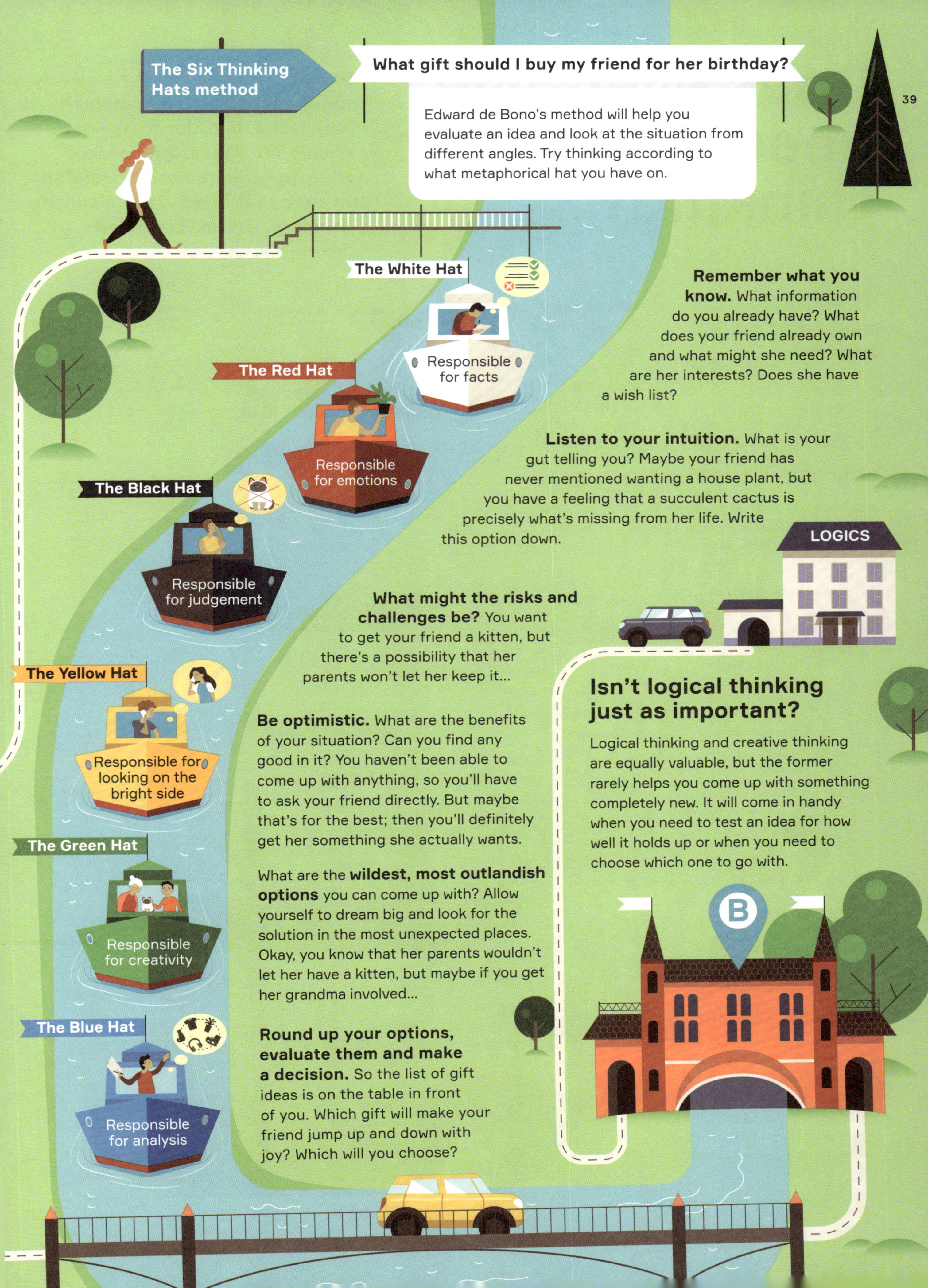

The Six Thinking Hats method

39

What gift should I buy my friend for her birthday?

Edward de Bono's method will help you evaluate an idea and look at the situation from different angles. Try thinking according to what metaphorical hat you have on.

The White Hat
Responsible for facts

The Red Hat
Responsible for emotions

The Black Hat
Responsible for judgement

The Yellow Hat
Responsible for looking on the bright side

The Green Hat
Responsible for creativity

The Blue Hat
Responsible for analysis

LOGICS

B

Remember what you know. What information do you already have? What does your friend already own and what might she need? What are her interests? Does she have a wish list?

Listen to your intuition. What is your gut telling you? Maybe your friend has never mentioned wanting a house plant, but you have a feeling that a succulent cactus is precisely what's missing from her life. Write this option down.

What might the risks and challenges be? You want to get your friend a kitten, but there's a possibility that her parents won't let her keep it...

Be optimistic. What are the benefits of your situation? Can you find any good in it? You haven't been able to come up with anything, so you'll have to ask your friend directly. But maybe that's for the best; then you'll definitely get her something she actually wants.

What are the wildest, most outlandish options you can come up with? Allow yourself to dream big and look for the solution in the most unexpected places. Okay, you know that her parents wouldn't let her have a kitten, but maybe if you get her grandma involved...

Round up your options, evaluate them and make a decision. So the list of gift ideas is on the table in front of you. Which gift will make your friend jump up and down with joy? Which will you choose?

Isn't logical thinking just as important?

Logical thinking and creative thinking are equally valuable, but the former rarely helps you come up with something completely new. It will come in handy when you need to test an idea for how well it holds up or when you need to choose which one to go with.

Does everyone need systematic thinking?

The older you get, the more clearly you will recognize the complexity of the world. In order to navigate difficult situations, it helps to notice how things are interrelated and keep that in mind when solving a problem. This skill is called "systematic thinking."

Thinking systematically means:

seeing the whole, not just the separate parts

noticing connections between parts

recognizing patterns in how a system works and making predictions about how it will manifest in the future

How do you spot a system?

A system consists of correlated elements that make up and work as a whole

All systems have:

- Elements
- Designated functions of parts
- Correlation

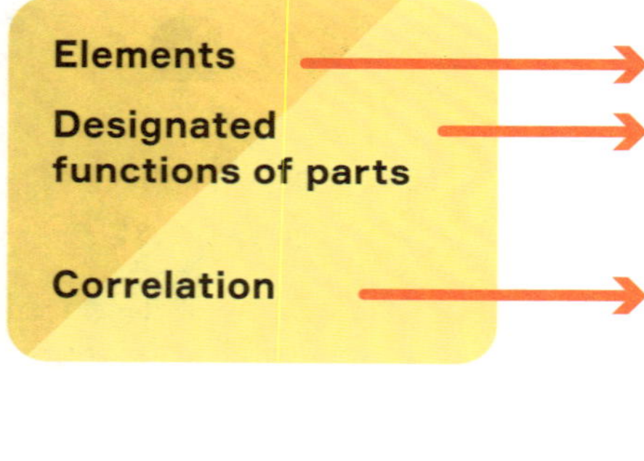

Ovule
Where the seeds are formed and stored

Flower
Organ of procreation; where the ovule and seeds are

Stem
Delivers the necessary particles to all parts of the plant

Leaves
Allows the plant to "breathe" and receive energy; necessary for growth and development

Roots
Absorb water and minerals from the earth

Flower

The plant's purpose is to reproduce

Field

If we look at our world as one big system, it looks a lot like a nesting doll.
Any system, whether it be a person, a plant, a machine, a story, etc., is made up of many single parts that come together to create one coherent whole.

Farm

Why should I think systematically?

see the connection between different events

get a "bird's-eye" view of a situation and look at it from different angles

think in terms of **"cause and effect"**

work in more complex, **fascinating professions**

look at the world with more confidence and make better choices

How can I learn to think systematically?

Read more, expand your horizons and learn something new every day.

Play, solve puzzles and brainteasers as well as problem-solve ("Theory of Inventive Problem Solving").

Deconstruct concepts and put the pieces together again. When you do this, you learn information about each working part and gain a better understanding of how the system functions.

Try new things, experiment, change up your routine.

Ask yourself a lot of "what if?" questions; make predictions and compare them with the actual outcomes.

Analyze events and try to find their causes (why did this happen?) and their effects (what did this lead to?). Make an effort to look at them from different perspectives. What did this event mean for each person involved?

How is a system structured?

Inside a system, everything is interconnected. So, if one component malfunctions or undergoes some kind of change, that will have an effect on all the other components. This is called a feedback loop.

In real life, a system doesn't react to change immediately:

It usually takes time before we can see the effect that a change has had on a system, and sometimes this change doesn't occur where we expect it to. In such cases, we might incorrectly identify the cause of something.

Cause: trying to protect crops

Pesticides don't just kill pests, they also kill bees.

This example demonstrates how our actions can lead to the opposite of our desired outcome. Therefore you can't always rely on things to be perfectly traceable to a clear cause.

Effect: crops were lost

Plants that aren't pollinated won't produce crops.

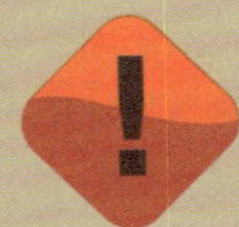

Important: *don't draw rash conclusions from an event. Observe and allow time to pass. Maybe you'll see that the event can be repeated with a completely different cause.*

How to save money, or what is a budget?

You want to buy a new bike, go to the amusement park with your classmates, see a new movie, order pizza, update your wardrobe... But how do you squeeze all those expenses into your allowance? You have to learn how to manage both your savings and your spending. How much money do you get each week, month, etc.? What fraction of it do you spend? How do you save money? How can you earn more?

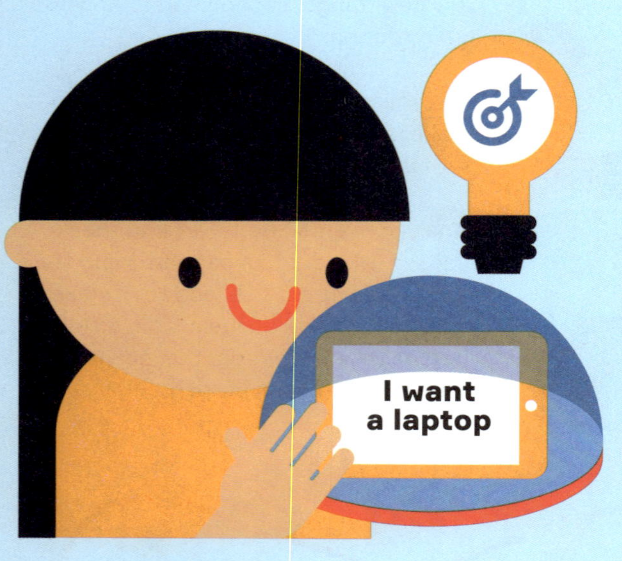

I want a laptop. How do I save up for it?

First and foremost, decide what you want most of all. Is it new running shoes, a laptop, a trip to the zoo perhaps?

Make a wish list. Find out how much each item costs and decide what your goal is for saving money.

This is your goal.

If you get an allowance or make money yourself, you already have:

Income
The money you get.

Expenses
The money you spend.

If you are making more money than you are spending, the remainder is your savings.

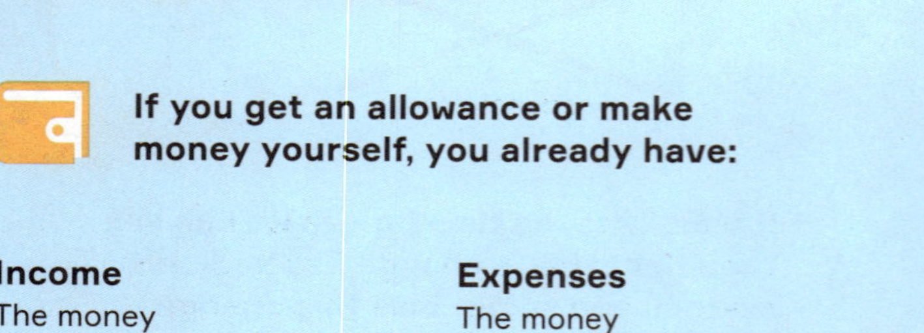

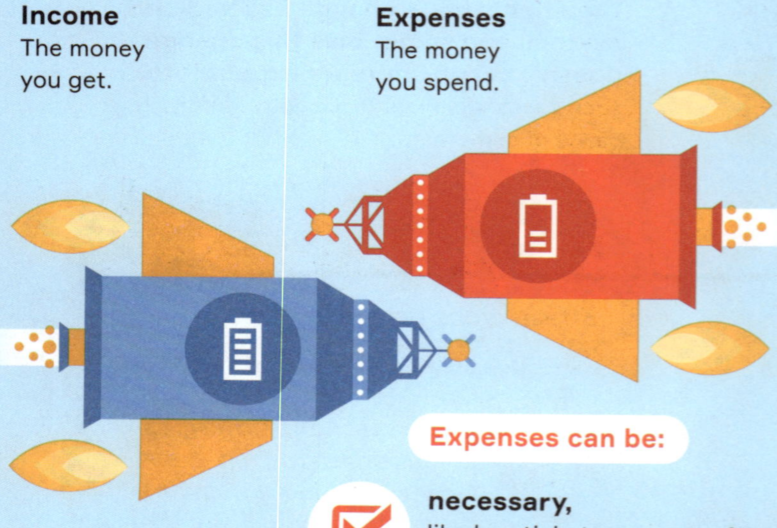

necessary,
like bus tickets or money for your phone

unnecessary,
like money you spend on movies or a new hat

Decrease your spending

How do I stop using my money for trivial things?

- **Keep a log of your purchases.** That way you'll have it all in front of you; you'll be able to see what you can cut back on to achieve your dream.

- **Don't impulse buy!** If you see something on the rack you'd like to take home with you, set it aside and think on it. Come back in a week to see if you still like it as much as you did before.

- **Set aside some of your allowance.** Decide which percentage of your allowance you want to save, and stick to it.

How do I make better use of my money?

- Look at ads and save coupons: the price for an item can be different depending on where you buy it.

- Ask your parents to set up a bank account for you. When you make a large purchase, use your card. A lot of banks give you cashback (the bank compensates for a portion of your purchase) and you can save quite a bit of money this way!

Keep your money on your card, rather than in cash inside of a wallet.

If your card gets stolen, **freeze your account immediately.**

Don't ever tell anyone your card number or any passwords. Even bank employees aren't allowed to ask this information!

Increase your earnings

It will take me ten years to save up for what I want with my allowance only. What can I do?

- **Get a part-time job.** You can legally work after turning 14.

- Ask your parents to **give you money as a gift** for an upcoming holiday.

- **Keep your savings in a savings account** instead of a piggy bank.

How does putting your money in a bank help?

A bank used to pay you interest for the ability to use your money. Nowdays a bank account can help you to save your money and manage it wisely by not spending it all at once.

How can I save money?

Don't let just anyone **borrow money from you;** make sure you trust the person.

Learn to spot **scammers.**

If your "friend" asks you for money through a text, call him back and **make sure his account wasn't hacked.**

What's next?

Think about:

These questions will help you understand yourself better. Come back to them once every couple of months.

- What difficulties do you encounter in your learning? How can you help yourself? What can you do better?
- Do you have enough time to do everything you want to do? Do you have time for rest? What can you change to make that time?
- Can you focus on just one thing at a time? Try counting how many times you look at your phone while doing your homework.
- What new, original ideas have you come up with that you can remember? Did you write them down? How did you come up with them?
- Do you question what others say to you, even adults? Or do you take it as fact?

What to read:

- **Getting Things Done for Teens: Take Control of Your Life in a Distracting World** by David Allen, Mike Williams, Mark Wallace

- **Super Student** by Olav Schewe

- **You're Smarter Than You Think: A Kid's Guide to Multiple Intelligences** by Thomas Armstrong

- **Rich Dad Poor Dad for Teens: The Secrets about Money — That You Don't Learn in School!** by Robert T. Kiyosaki

Your tools:

- Calendar
- "To-do", "projects", and "someday" lists
- Alarm clock or timer
- App or notebook to keep track of your budget

What to watch:

Inside the mind of a master procrastinator
by Tim Urban

Science is for everyone, kids included by Beau Lotto and Amy O'Toole

CHAPTER 3

My feelings and I

- What is emotional intelligence?

- What emotions do I experience?

- What should I do with my feelings?

- I don't know how to handle failure

- What's next?

What is emotional intelligence?

When we hear the word "intelligence," our mind immediately goes to solving complex math problems and getting the answers right on a test (IQ). We're often ignorant of the existence of other types of intelligence, such as emotional intelligence (EQ).

But what's more important: IQ or EQ?

Our **intelligence quotient (IQ)** helps us acquire knowledge and use it.

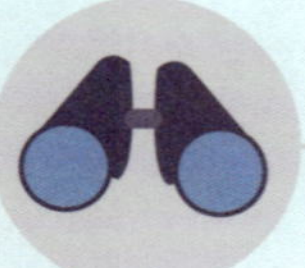

Our **emotional quotient (EQ)** is a measure of how well we're able to relate to and interact with ourselves and others.

Emotional intelligence is the ability to recognize and understand your emotions and the emotions of others, and adjust your behavior accordingly.

Why do we need emotional intelligence?

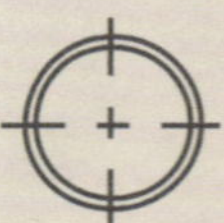

Recognizing emotions
Understanding what you're feeling and why.

Regulating emotions
The ability to look at your emotions from an outside perspective and allow them to exist.

Empathy
Because you understand what people are feeling, you can show them compassion and help them deal with their feelings.

Why do we need to understand our feelings?

When you're overwhelmed by a feeling, you react immidiately. When you're in this state, you might unknowingly hurt yourself or others. Things that elicit a strong emotional response are called "triggers." Everyone has his or her own set of triggers determined by his or her personal history. Making sense of your own feelings will allow you to recognize those triggers and manage your reaction to them.

Why do we need to understand other people's feelings?

One of the markers of a high level of emotional intelligence is empathy, or the ability to feel and understand what someone else is feeling, even if you've never gone through it yourself. Yet simply making sense of our own feelings is difficult, so why should we bother with those of others? The thing is that any deep, genuine human connections (love, friendship, familial bonds) are built on empathy. Empathy allows people to truly connect with each other and work towards mutual goals.

So what level is my emotional intelligence at?

Low level
You get caught in the tide of your emotions. You feel powerless to your anger, pain and frustration. You can't even explain what it is exactly that you're feeling.

Medium level
You understand what you're feeling and are able to accept it, but sometimes you get consumed by your emotions and have a hard time getting out of that state.

High level
You recognize and accept your feelings, and you're able to release the unpleasant ones.

How can I work on my emotional intelligence?

1

Observe your emotions from afar.
Ask yourself: What am I feeling? You can start a journal specifically for this purpose. Write down your observations. What upset you? What made you happy? Why did you get mad?

2

Observe other people's feelings.
Consider what might have caused someone to act the way he or she did. Put yourself in the person's shoes. Show empathy and compassion. Talk to your close friends about your feelings and listen to them talk about theirs.

4

Try to identify your "triggers" — what causes your strongest emotional reactions. Talk to people whom you trust and who can manage their emotions skillfully.

3

Play with perspective. Change the lens through which you view the world, from "rose-tinted glasses" to "sunglasses": play around with viewing an experience in a positive light and then in a completely negative one.

What emotions do I experience?

A great tool for identifying your feelings is Robert Plutchik's wheel of emotions.

How is this wheel structured?

Joy

When we experience joy, we gain a newfound sense of meaning. Pay attention to what brings you joy in order to learn more about yourself and what's truly important to you. Joy is also a big source of power and positive energy; it gives you the "fuel" necessary to take on great projects and climb metaphorical mountains, and also to simply get through the day.

Fear

Everybody feels afraid from time to time. However unpleasant it may be, fear can also be useful. It will make you think twice before standing on the edge of a cliff. But there are also irrational fears that hold you back, like the fear of failure, which prevents you from fulfilling your potential. What are you afraid of? Is this fear rational or not?

Surprise

The most fleeting of feelings, it comes unexpectedly (obviously) and leaves in a flash. There are people who love being surprised, and those that are uncomfortable with the feeling (no surprise parties for the latter). Both reactions are very normal.

Sadness

All people have their reasons for being sad. Paying attention to what brings it on for you will also lead you to what might alleviate it. For many, this is the time and source of creativity. Try to express how you feel with a poem or a guitar riff. This is also when you may need the most support. Is there someone you can talk openly to in times like these?

Anger

Under the umbrella of anger sits a wide range of feelings, from irritation (a small bonfire) to uncontrollable rage (a full-fledged wildfire). Anger is the other emotion that provides you with a lot of energy. This energy can be used to work towards something that puts your anger to good use. On the other hand, bottling up your feelings of anger can lead to explosive aggression.

Pay attention to what feelings you experience throughout the day. What emotions come up most when you're at school? At home?

The center of the wheel holds the most intense version of an emotion. As you zoom out, the emotion gets less and less intense.

For example:

grief — the most severe of the three

sadness — medium severity

pensiveness — the least severe

In between two "petals" are combination emotions, which are born from those on each side of them.

When trust meets joy, love is born. When trust and fear combine, they breed submission.

joy +
trust =
love

What should I do with my feelings?

Okay, great, now you know that there is a ton of different feelings — but what do you do when they arrive? It's true that your feelings affect your thoughts and actions in major ways. If you don't want your feelings to control you, you need to learn to control them.

How can I get to know my feelings better?

Don't label a feeling as "good" or "bad." All feelings serve a purpose. Just try to recognize them.

Write them down. Then you'll have a better understanding of what really affects you and why.

Notice what you feel when consuming media (reading a book or watching a movie).

Ask yourself: **Where do I feel this in my body?**

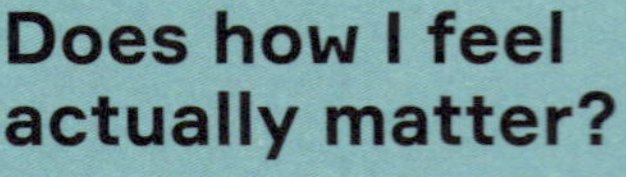

Does how I feel actually matter?

According to numerous studies, constantly experiencing negative emotions has a negative effect on our health. Meanwhile, positive emotions help you live a longer and better life.

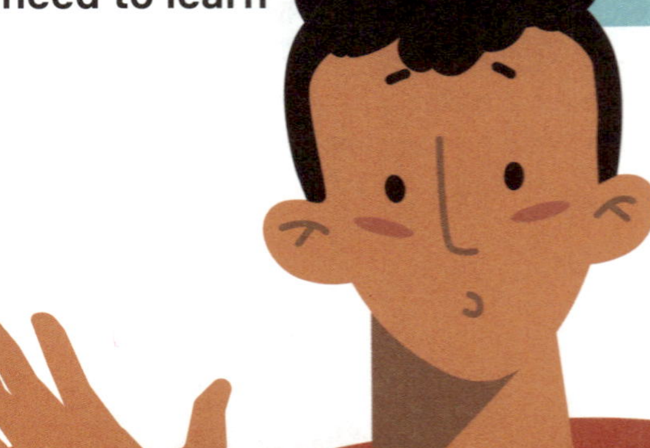

What can I do when I feel overwhelmed by a negative feeling?

Staying above water and not letting yourself get sucked under is achieved by practicing **the technique of letting go:**

1 **Determine what it is exactly you are feeling.** Don't scold or judge yourself and don't shame yourself for it. Feelings are an inherent part of being human.

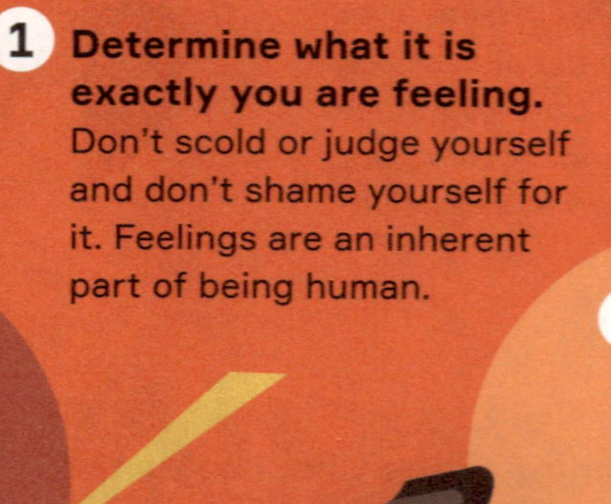

2 **Allow yourself to feel what you're feeling.** Don't try to change it. Say to yourself, "I feel embarrassed. That's normal. Hello, embarrassment."

Something you can do to center yourself and gain perspective is to meditate. Meditation isn't magic, nor is it just for monks; it's a way of training your mind. It helps you regain focus, clear your head and separate yourself from what's going on inside you. Like any other type of training, it gets easier each time you do it. If focusing on your breathing just isn't working, try to focus on something else, like a clock arrow or the sounds around you. Do what works best for you.

A simple meditation
Try to keep this going for a minute; you can increase the time as you gain experience.

1 Breathe.

2 Feel your breath in your body (the tingling around your nostrils, the rise and fall of your stomach, your heartbeat speeding up and slowing down).

3 If you notice yourself getting distracted, simply return to breathing.

4 Don't beat yourself up for losing focus. Instead, be patient.

5 You can count the number of your inhales and exhales to 10 and then start over.

Becoming a spectator of your feelings

It's easier to understand and accept your feelings when you don't play an active part in them. So practice acting as a bystander, curious yet impartial.

Ask yourself questions. You came home from school absolutely furious. Try to figure out what caused you to feel that way: was it the C you got from the teacher who grades too harshly? Was the grade really unfair or are you mad at yourself for not putting in more work? Would your reaction change if you accepted your part in the bad grade?

Have an outside perspective. Imagine if what you are experiencing happened to your close friend. What advice would you give her? How would you support her?

3 **Notice the accompanying physical sensations.** Ask yourself questions such as, "Where do I feel this in my body? What is the sensation like? Can I live with this sensation?" Treat your discomfort with gentle and loving curiosity.

4 **Demonstrate love.** Treat your unpleasant emotion as you would a crying baby; nurture it, care for it. Say, "I'm here. I'm with you. I love you and I hear you. This feeling has a place in my life. It won't last forever; this too shall pass." It's ok to hold your own hand or hug yourself for support.

I don't know how to handle failure

Something didn't work out the way you planned? You worked hard at something but didn't see any results? It's easy to allow defeats such as these to make you feel like a failure and stop you from trying again. There are those, however, who see failure as a way to learn, who are even motivated by it to keep pushing forward. How do they do it?

Stumbling blocks are full of possibility

Someties, failure turns you away from an opportunity in order to redirect you to a new and better one.

Mistakes show us the chinks in our armor or the flaws in our approach. They do so to help us improve in the areas we struggle in and work on our weaknesses.

Ever heard the phrase: What doesn't kill you makes you stronger? Mistakes are there to teach us to accept that things won't always go according to plan. They assure us that there will be challenges we must face in order to get what we want.

What should I do when things don't go my way?

Try to stay cool and keep a positive attitude.

Be objective and focus on what you can control, rather than fretting about that which you can't.

Don't worry about what anyone might think or say. Remember that this is just a bump in the road and you're going to have many successes in the future.

Your how-to guide for handling hurdles

When faced with a challenge on your way to success, the **actions you take** and the **attitude you have** are equally important.

Let's say you had a competition and totally blew it; you were hoping to get first place but didn't even come in third. There's nothing you can do about the outcome of the race now. What matters is how you react and what you choose to do next.

Meet the challenge head-on

Maybe you didn't get enough practice in. Call up a friend and invite him to train with you; it might be more fun and seem less daunting than doing it alone.

Focus on the process, not the outcome

Don't think about how hard it is to win nationals. Think about how much you love the sport and how much you enjoy doing it. You can aim for gold within your region first, and then work your way toward bigger goals.

Don't give up if you don't see immediate results

You've been training hard for a few weeks, but your coach still says your skills aren't where they need to be. You might get frustrated and discouraged, but don't give up. You're only at the start of your journey.

Take a creative approach

Think outside the box when looking for a solution. If you like basketball, but you don't have skills and motivation to learn the sport, maybe joining the cheerleading squad is the best option for you?

Try to be objective and keep your feelings in check

Don't lash out at your coach or your teammates or blame anyone for your defeat. Try to find the real, unbiased reason for what happened. Breathe, calm yourself down and take an objective look at the problem.

Focus on what you can control

You can't go back in time and win your last race, and maybe you're just not in the right shape yet to get first place. That's okay. What you can do is get more hours in and show better results.

Listen to yourself and your intuition first and foremost

Regardless of what anybody else says, only you know your situation, so it's up to you to figure out what went wrong.

Be flexible and prepared to back down when it's time

Sometimes you really can't do anything about a situation. If you've tried long and hard and it's still not happening, it might be time to consider that the path just isn't right for you. Apply your energy somewhere else, somewhere you can truly shine.

What's next?

Think about:

These questions will help you understand yourself better.
Come back to them once every couple of months.

- What emotions do you feel throughout the day?
  Pause for a moment and name the prevailing emotion that
  you're experiencing right now.
- What feelings associated with past events visit you often?
  Observe them, name them, notice how they reverberate in
  your body.
- Do you notice any particular emotions in the people
  who surround you? What causes these feelings? How do
  they react to their feelings? How can you support them
  and help them cope?

What to read:

- **101 Ways to Conquer Teen Anxiety: Simple Tips,
  Techniques and Strategies for Overcoming
  Anxiety, Worry and Panic Attacks** by Jon Patrick
  Hatcher and Thomas McDonagh

- **Emotional Intelligence: Why It Can Matter More
  Than IQ** by Daniel Goleman

Your tools:

- Diary
- Mood tracker

What to watch:

Are there universal expressions of emotion? by Sophie Zadeh

How to make stress your friend by Kelly McGonigal

CHAPTER 4

Socializing

- **Should I tell the truth or not?**

- **How can I truly listen?**

- **Coming to an agreement**

- **What if people judge me?**

- **How do I share my ideas?**

- **Public speaking**

- **How can I write well?**

- **What's next?**

Should I tell the truth or not?

Sometimes we lie on impulse, barely noticing it. Other times we feel like we have no choice, like the truth is too damaging and dangerous. What should we do instead?

Imagine: you went to see a movie with your friends, and left the movie theater completely disappointed. You turn to your friends and see that they're all raving about how much they loved it. What will you do? Will you agree with them, express your opinion or keep quiet?

When are we tempted to lie?

When we want to conceal something shameful

When we want to embellish and exaggerate

When we want to avoid an uncomfortable situation

When we want someone to like us or simply don't want to offend, disappoint or upset someone close to us

If we lie, what happens?

You could lose somebody's trust. If you catch someone in a lie, you're going to have a hard time trusting the person wholly and completely in the future. Even if the person lied just once and it was told with good intentions.

Lying takes a lot of strength and energy. It's easy for a lie to snowball out of control. A liar has to remember exactly what he said and to whom and, in some cases, he must constantly keep filling in holes in his story.

You start becoming mistrustful yourself. The more you lie, the more you will suspect those around you as being liars. It's a way of justifying your actions. It doesn't matter if everybody lies, right?

Silence Island

You can just keep your lips sealed. After all, no one can force us to speak our minds or disclose all that we know. But staying silent is also a choice with consequences.

If the person you're hiding the truth from has a right to know it, and if your silence will deceive or blindside her, then this is no different from lying.

Your mom decides to take you out to dinner to celebrate your finishing the school year with straight A's on your report card. Only, you failed to mention that you got a C in geography...

You found out about another classmate's secret and are keeping it from your best friend. Your silence will not affect your friend's behavior as this secret has nothing to do with her.

Deceptive to others ☹

Not deceptive to others ☺

Truth Island

Most of the time, people's feelings are hurt not by what you say, but by how you say it. The truth doesn't have to be harsh or tactless. It's important to say it in a way that will make it easier to receive, thus more effective.

Unnecessarily harsh:
You failed the audition because you can't sing.

Carefully and considerately phrased:
You're very artistic. I think that, if you work more on your vocals, you can totally get into next year's play, maybe even the musical.

If it's really hard for you to be honest, ask yourself:

- How will this lie affect the other person?
- What will she feel when she finds out I've lied to her?
- Am I willing to violate this person's trust and our relationship?

Remember:

- Being honest doesn't mean being rude or hurtful.
- Your opinion is exactly that, not a universal or indisputable truth.
- When you're honest, you give a person the opportunity to look at the situation through your eyes, and that might help.

What if I quit lying altogether?

Things will become so much simpler. Because speaking the truth means being true to yourself in any company and situation.

How can I truly listen?

We don't even realize how much time we spend talking. We have conversations with teachers, classmates, parents, siblings, friends, etc. But when we engage in these conversations, how well do we listen to what the other person is saying?

Hearing isn't the same as listening. What's the difference?

Hearing is one of our five senses; it's not voluntary. But listening means actively engaging with the other person.

Yet, sometimes, while talking to another person, we don't actually pay attention to what she is saying. We let it go in one ear and out the other and anxiously wait for the right time to interject with our own thoughts. Sound familiar? We also don't listen if we're upset, tired or bored.

A good listener is someone who is attentive, doesn't interrupt and tries to understand what the other person is saying. People value good listeners and open up to them because they feel like you genuinely care.

no one confides in me

people don't want to engage with me

I can't compromise or come to any agreements

I don't receive new information

people share their ideas and observations with me

people like talking to me

I can easily find the middle ground

I'm always learning new things from others

I DON'T KNOW HOW TO LISTEN

I KNOW HOW TO LISTEN

When should I not listen?

- If somebody is judging you as a person instead of your actions.
- If the other person doesn't respect your feelings or point of view.
- If you're being threatened.
- If you're being blamed.

How do I become a better listener?

1

Don't rush to express your own opinion or make judgements about what someone is saying.

2

Be respectful of the other person's opinions and beliefs, even if they don't line up with your own.

3

Pay close attention to what the other person is saying.

4

Help steer the conversation by asking relevant questions.

5

Be empathetic by showing the other person compassion and support.

Why should you ask questions?

When you ask questions, you can take the conversation in a new direction, or dig deeper into the subject by helping the other person remember details and look at the situation with a fresh view.

If the conversation comes to a halt, hold back on immediately making it about yourself. Ask another question instead.

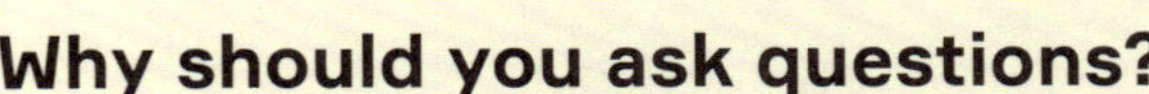

HOW DO I ASK A GOOD QUESTION?

Questions can be

closed-ended

open-ended

Closed-ended questions expect a "yes" or "no" answer. These types of questions don't open the floor for discussion and are, therefore, a dead end.

✖ Do you like the new teacher?

✖ Are you friends with Sanjay?

✖ Are you gonna go out after school?

Open-ended questions start with words like "why," "what," "where," "how," etc. They make the speaker think about her answer and can be replied to in a number of ways. Questions such as these allow us to learn way more than closed-ended questions do.

↑ What do you think of the new teacher?

↑ Who are you friends with in class?

↑ What are your plans for after school?

Coming to an agreement

You've been a haggler for as long as you can remember — either begging your parents to let you go out with your friends or to buy you a new bike. These weren't merely discussions, they were negotiations, and the outcome depended on how you went about asking and coming to an agreement.

What types of negotiations are there?

At the heart of any negotiation lies a conflict of interest. In order to resolve the conflict, the participants try to make some sort of deal.

Win — lose. These arguments resemble a tug-of-war match: each participant pulls and pulls in his or her own direction. If one person gains an advantage, it happens at the expense of the other person's wishes. There is only one winner.

Lose — lose. Both parties relent on more and more of their terms, just so the conflict can be over and done with. Or the complete opposite happens; they start to do everything just to spite the other, with the mentality of "If I don't win, then nobody does." Both people lose.

Win — win. The two parties don't waste their energy battling with each other, instead choosing to collaborate and become allies. They focus on solving the problem rather than who's right and who's wrong, and both end up winning.

Types of debaters by Gavin Kennedy

Their main objective is to get their way, so they end up being inflexible and deaf to reason. An argument involving someone with this mentality is doomed from the start.

Give in to any and all demands, allowing themselves to be walked all over so as to keep the peace and prevent any harm from coming to the relationship. They almost always end up losing.

Sly, cunning, and willing to play dirty, usually playing on the weaknesses of the donkey and the sheep types. They leave their morals at the door and do whatever it takes to win.

They respect the person they're talking to, think in terms of the big picture and aim to build long-lasting relationships, don't lie or manipulate.

How do I make sure no one loses?

Figure out the nature of the conflict and what each side really wants

When trying to find a solution, stop and look at the person in front of you. Consider her interests lie, how she is feeling. Make an effort to truly listen to her. Find out what the real issue is. You can help the process by asking open-ended questions: "what," "why," "how," "who," etc.

Come up with a number of solutions

Now that you know what each person wants, it's time to figure out how to make it happen. Brainstorm as many possible solutions as you can.

Choose the option that satisfies both of you

Talk about your options. You've already made great progress by hearing each other out and now have an understanding of your true desires, while managing to keep the conversation friendly. Thanks to these efforts, finding a mutually beneficial solution will come easily, without conflict or hurt feelings.

When trying to come to an agreement, it's easy to slip into a power struggle and try to get the upper hand (win-lose). But conversations such as these are only effective when everyone's wishes are taken into consideration (win-win).

But what if the other side refuses to be civil?

Your counterpart is being rude and insulting. You're feeling attacked and want to give her a taste of her own medicine. The proper way to act in this situation is to not stoop to her level. **Don't let yourself be provoked,** and remember that the outcome should depend on the points she makes, not the manner in which she says them.

Threats are never okay when solving a problem. If you're expecting to build a relationship with this person, **never resort to threatening or pressuring** her during an argument. Threats will spoil a good relationship and worsen a bad one.

Threats and pressure aren't always verbal; people may try to intimidate you with status and outward appearance. But having a fancy wrist watch and a rich dad doesn't make them right. **Don't pay any mind to these "special effects."**

What if people judge me?

Whether we like it or not, people judge us, our words and our actions constantly. As difficult as it may be to hear, criticism can be constructive and help you grow. We can choose to let someone's remark upset us and make us feel bad about ourselves, or we can think it over and use it to improve.

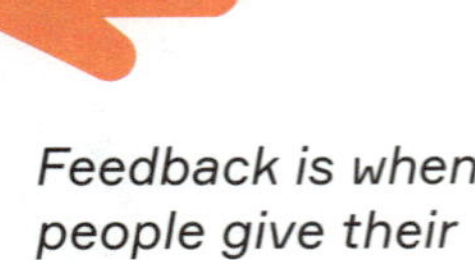

Feedback is when people give their opinion about something that you did or said.

We might ask for feedback, for example when we want to know how well we did on an assigned task.

Other times, people comment on your actions completely unwarrantedly. Take a moment and ask yourself what their intentions were: were they trying to hurt your feelings or to help you grow?

How do I accept criticism?

Before the conversation

Think about the goal of this conversation. What do you want from your peer: honest advice or validation?

During the conversation

Hear the person out. Try to see the situation and yourself through his or her eyes. Ask yourself why he or she thinks or feels that way.

Share your opinion. Another person's perspective is limited, just like yours. Getting both sides of the story will help you get a better picture and piece together the truth.

Don't let the conversation turn into an argument. Imagine that you're watching from the sidelines. What will allow you to grow the most? In which scenario do you learn something: when you react impulsively and emotionally, or when you're able to listen and take into account a different point of view and think it over?

After the conversation

Take action. If you agree with the feedback, start changing your behavior.

Try something new. Sometimes we aren't sure if we should take the advice we're given. Try it out anyway; you're not risking much, but could really gain something from the experience.

Don't give in. When we step out of our comfort zone, we're bound to make a few mistakes. Even if you mess up, don't get discouraged; positive results are just around the corner.

What gets in the way of our accepting criticism?

It's often that our emotional response and denial stop us from being able to take criticism.

Course of action

We don't think it's true

Your friend thanks you for letting her borrow your bike, but comments offhandedly that you might want to change the seat, because it's stiff and uncomfortable.

Find out why the other person believes this.

Don't let your feelings get in the way of listening to a different perspective.

We don't consider the other person credible

A mom tells her daughter that her clothes don't go together. The daughter thinks: What does she know about modern fashion?

Remember that an outside perspective can be more objective.

Try to take away something valuable from any feedback you get.

Another person's words make us insecure

A student does a presentation in front of the class. The teacher calls out from the back of the room, "Speak up! I can barely hear you!" Some people might get embarrassed and finish their talk early. And others will listen to the teacher, raise their volume and give a great presentation.

Remember: pobody's nerfect!

Don't be afraid to make mistakes.

Use feedback as a catalyst for improvement.

When should we ignore criticism?

Don't pay any attention to it if:

You're being held to unrealistic standards

You're being threatened

People are judging you as a person and not your actions

Your feelings and experiences aren't being respected

You're being blamed for everything that went wrong

How should I share my ideas?

Coming up with something new and cool is only the first step. Then you have to make your idea be heard. So many brilliant ideas never see the light of day because they weren't presented properly. Sharing your ideas is a skill, just like any other.

Why should I learn how to present my ideas?

Everyone gets ideas, not just scientist-inventor-geniuses.

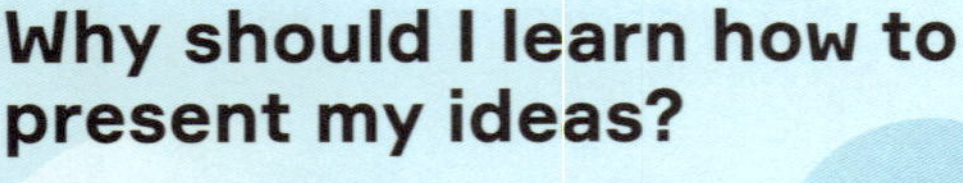

You're always coming up with them: when you propose starting a book club in school, when you suggest a good film to your friends, when you try to talk your parents into getting a dog…

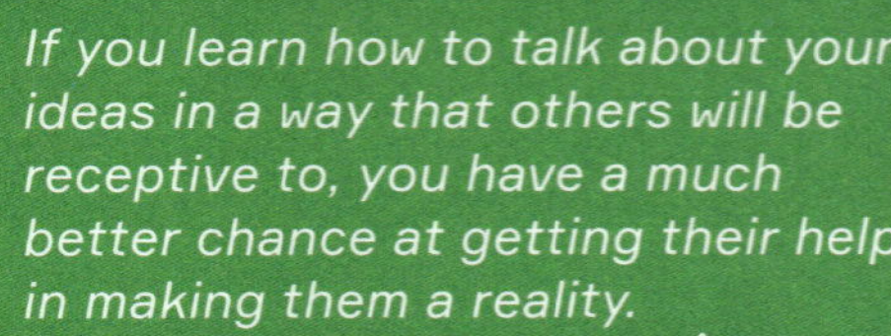

If you learn how to talk about your ideas in a way that others will be receptive to, you have a much better chance at getting their help in making them a reality.

Why is it hard to put an idea into words?

The billionaire writer, J. K. Rowling, was turned down by 12 publishing houses until one finally took a chance on her work and printed the first Harry Potter book.

As soon as you open your mouth, your idea begins its obstacle course. The person you're talking to might criticize it, talk over you or change the topic altogether.

Your audience's attention can be affected by a number of things that have nothing to do with the idea: their mood, the environment, the sound of your voice, etc.

If your idea is rejected, that doesn't mean it's a bad idea. Don't get discouraged and try again. Maybe your counterpart just wasn't in the right headspace to listen.

Why are some ideas memorable, while others aren't?

You show viral videos to your friends and post them in your stories, but you don't give your teacher's lecture a second thought. That's how ideas work, too. Some capture our attention and live in our minds, while others die.

According to Chip and Dan Heath an idea "sticks" if:

It draws attention

It's easy to understand and remember

People agree with it and believe in it

It evokes an emotional reaction

It can be transformed into a reality

How can I catch people's attention and make them remember?

State your idea in simple terms
Transform your idea into something your audience will understand: simple and close to your audience's interests. Sometimes a proverb can say it best: brevity is clarity.

Tell a story
Stories are powerful. They bring concepts to life by allowing the listener to imagine himself as part of the plot, to experience it from within.

Add details and examples
Help your listeners remember by giving examples that demonstrate your point. Raw numbers aren't all that memorable by themselves.

Make them feel something
When something resonates with us emotionally, that seals the deal. Even anger is better than indifference.

Support your idea
Get your stamp of approval from someone trusted and respected, like a parent, a relative, a teacher or an expert.

Break the mold
People remember the unexpected, the out-of-the-ordinary. Make a joke, ask a riddle, do something that will spark their curiosity. It will not only help you get their attention, but keep it too.

Public speaking

A big part of sharing your ideas is the ability to perform. No one comes out of the womb being magically good at public speaking. If you train yourself and prepare for your speeches and presentations, peforming in front of large audiences will become second nature to you.

How should I act when I'm giving a speech?

Speak loudly and clearly
If nobody can hear what you're saying, then you're wasting your time.

Show and tell
Show pictures, photos, graphs, etc. to give your audience some variety. This is meant to keep them engaged and to make your presentation more memorable.

Don't rush
Feeling nervous can cause you to speak more quickly, which will wear out your listeners and cause you to lose their attention just as quickly. Pause to accentuate importance and create space for your listeners to think over what you have just said.

Structuring your speech
Your speech should resemble climbing a mountain.

At the foot of the mountain (introduction)
Prepare the listeners and establish a relationship with them. You can do this by:
- Sharing a relevant fun fact
- Asking a question
- Telling a joke
- Telling them a little about yourself

What will help me to be a better public speaker?

1 Read more
Reading helps you get accustomed to proper written language. And when you discuss things you have read, you get better at conveying complex ideas verbally.

2 Read out loud and recite interesting texts in front of your loved ones
Switch places — ask them to do the same for you. That way you'll judge their performance and learn from it as well as from your own.

3 Perform plays and improvise with your family during family gatherings
Come up with stories, poems and songs and put on a show.

4 Join a drama club

The climb (the meat of your presentation)

Give an overview of the issue and explain why this is something your listeners should care about. Sprinkle in examples, statistics, arguments. This will show your audience that you know what you're talking about.

At the peak (the climax)

In two to three sentences, sum up and emphasize your main point — the most important message you're trying to convey.

The descent (conclusion)

Finish your presentation off with:

- Briefly reiterate your points
- Restate the main idea
- Thank your listeners for their time and attention
- Leave your audience with something to think about

What should I do if...

I'm nervous

Feeling nervous before a performance is totally normal. To cope with it, take a walk, shake out your hands, stretch your wrists and fingers. Movement allows your nervous system to calm down. Taking a couple slow, deep breaths will also help.

Nobody's listening

Your audience's attention has worn thin; they're probably feeling bored. Shake this up and draw back their attention by making a joke or asking an unexpected question.

I don't know how to answer a tough question

Thank the person who asked the question and promise to look into the subject and get back to him or her later.

I forget what I was saying

No problem — it happens to everyone. Say honestly, "I lost my train of thought," and back-track a little to regain your direction.

How should I prepare for a performance?

 **Write exactly what you will say in your speech beforehand** and commit it to memory. When you feel confident that you know your material, convert it into short bullet-points (main thoughts). Use those to practice and keep track of where you're heading.

 **Rehearse the speech in front of your friends and family** until you can recite it without hesitating, meandering and stumbling over your words.

 **Record your speech on audio or video.** Listen/watch through with someone you trust, then analyze and correct your mistakes.

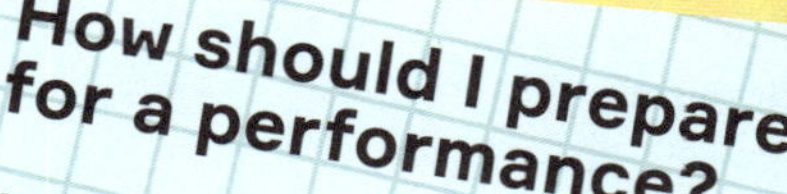
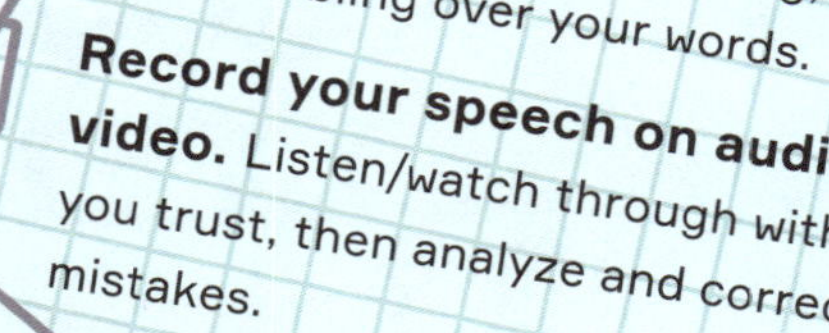

How can I write well?

There are rules and structure in writing that help you express your thoughts clearly and effectively. Applying these rules will help you write research papers, letters, essays and even posts on your social media accounts.

Keep in mind, these points apply to non-fiction writing. Creative writing is an entirely different world that has its own, separate rules.

Why do you write?

Before writing something, you must understand the purpose of your words. The end result should hold value for both the writer and the readers.

Report

Learn something new and share that knowledge with the class.

Essay

Master the art of expressing your opinion, structuring your thoughts and analyzing material in written form.

Social media or blog post

Entertain your friends, share life hacks and attract attention.

What is writing comprised of?

Words

Words are the building blocks of speech and writing. Each word you use must be purposeful, i.e., it must aid in conveying your main idea. If a word is unnecessary, cut it from your writing.

Sentences

A sentence should flow as effortlessly as if it was conversational speech. Don't overcomplicate your text, instead write simply.

Paragraphs with and without headings

Paragraphs are a means of compartmentalizing information so it makes the most sense. They instill order and break down long texts. Start your paragraphs with your main thought and some "hook."

Title

A title conveys the central meaning of the work. If a part of your writing can't be connected to your title, then it's either off-topic, or your title isn't doing its job.

Introduction

Introduces the readers to the topic and sparks interest in said topic.

Body paragraphs

Consist of arguments and reasoning that are interconnected in a way that makes sense.

Conclusion

Repeats the main idea, includes final thoughts and conclusions drawn from the text, as well as food for further thought.

How to write?

3

Research time! Find information, such as facts, stories, statistics and examples that help you construct your narrative and support your point of view.

4

Determine the order. What will you talk about in the beginning, middle and end? What makes the most sense?

5

The take-away. Don't forget to provide your readers with some sort of lesson learned to ensure they remember exactly what you wanted to convey.

2

Determine the central idea. Narrow your topic down. Decide where you stand and what exactly you want to express in your writing.

1

Find your topic. What interests you? What's been on your mind? What do you want to learn more and teach others about?

A WHITE BLANK PAGE, AND A SWELLING RA-A-AGE!!!

Just like with everything else, writing something is hard to start, even when you're knowledgeable about the topic and excited to share. Here are some tips for dealing with writer's block.

Simply write. You can't edit a blank page, so just get on it! Even if your first draft is terrible, it's much better than nothing. So jot down everything that comes to mind and worry about quality later.

Make a plan. Divide up the information and decide what goes where. Create the skeleton of your passage.

Write the text and then structure it. Or do it the other way around! Write your body paragraphs, which consist of your main thoughts, bolstered by evidence and analysis, and then add the introduction and conclusion to it.

Proofreading and editing

Read what you wrote over and make changes to improve it. Make sure that:

- ✓ Your text and title connect to your theme
- ✓ The order makes sense and conveys your thoughts in a systematic fashion
- ✓ Everything is interconnected (be especially careful with your intro and conclusion!)
- ✓ Your paragraphs divide the text into ideas
- ✓ Your text is easy to read and not unnecessarily complicated or long-winded

What's next?

Think about:

These questions will help you understand yourself better. Come back to them once every couple of months.

- Do you talk or listen more?
- What is your approach in an argument: do whatever it takes to get your way; give in to what the other person wants; or try to find a solution that benefits you both?
- Do you respond poorly to criticism? Why? Do you think perhaps you could take something out of it instead?
- Are you able to explain your thoughts on the first try?
- Have you ever spoken in front of an audience? How did it go? What can you do to improve for next time?

What to read:

- **How to be a Young #Writer** by Christopher Edge and Padhraic Mulholland

Your tools:

- Books
- Laptop or desktop
- Apps for making presentations (PowerPoint, Google Slides, Canva)
- Apps for drawing and graphing ideas (Figma, Canva)
- Phone with a camera or a voice recorder to tape your rehearsals

What to watch:

How to speak so that people want to listen
by Julian Treasure

TED's secret to great public speaking by
Chris Anderson

Relationships

- **Why do I need friends?**

- **How do I work in a team?**

- **How do I understand my parents and help them understand me?**

- **Dreaming of love**

- **What's next?**

Why do I need friends?

Ever heard the phrase, "You are the common denominator of the five people you spend the most time with?" If there's truth to this saying, then you should be very selective with your friends and not hesitate to invest time and energy into building positive relationships.

How can I tell if a friendship is genuine?

Real friendships are built on trust, authenticity and care. Don't wait for someone to demonstrate these qualities to you. Take the first step by showing compassion, giving support, being excited for your friends and inquiring about their interests. And do it genuinely, without expecting anything in return!

Real friendships are mutual.

How do I act so that people want to be friends with me?

Mark if you agree:

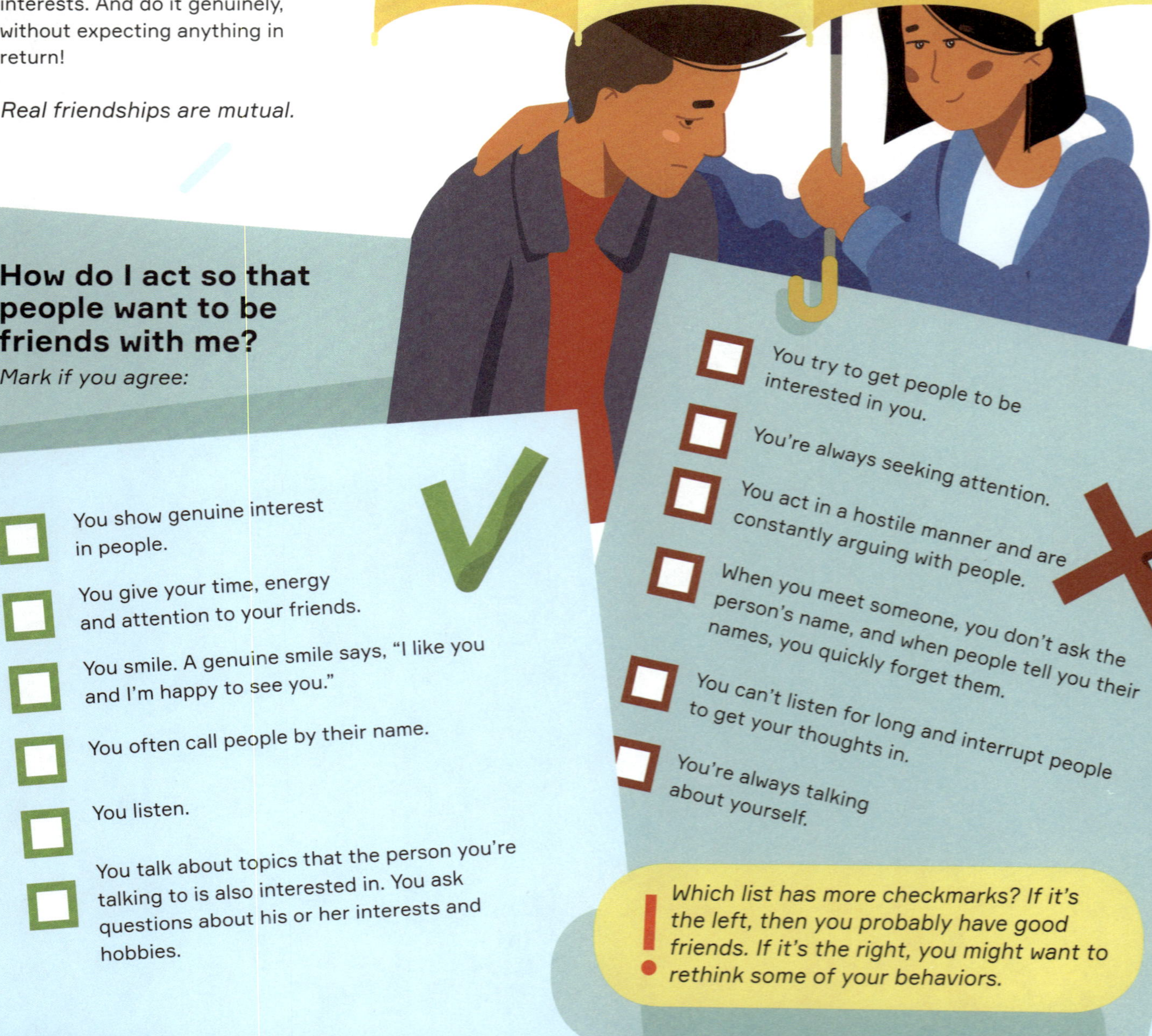

What affect do our friends have on us?

Shared ambitions and values
Which goals and beliefs do you share with your friends, and where do you differ?

Support system
If your friend has a fight with her parents, will you talk to him or her to help her feel better?

Behavior
Who inspired you to start playing sports, whose style did you integrate into yours, who introduced you to your favorite song?

We choose with whom we surround ourselves.

Our friends shape us as people.

Not just our friends, but even our friends' friends, even those we haven't met.

Friend or acquaintance?

- Usually, people have a few real friends, and the rest are acquaintances.

- Acquaintances are often people you meet or hang out with in school or at work, but with whom you won't make an effort to stay in touch during the summer.

- You're on good terms with your acquaintances, but you aren't close. You talk about what movies just came out, like each other's posts on Instagram, but don't reach out to them when you need someone.

- You confide in your friends but not your acquaintances; acquaintance relationships are often rooted in convenience.

Not a friend

- Never texts or calls first.

- Only reaches out to you when he or she needs something from you.

- Uses you if you have something he or she needs: money, possessions or connections.

- Is possessive and demands all of your attention; tears you away from your hobbies and other friendships.

- Always lets you down.

Remember: treat others the way you want to be treated.

How do I work in a team?

Why are we stronger together?

Collaboration is an amazing way to tackle large, daunting and important projects, whether it be in school or in your personal life. But it's not always easy to work with others. How can we excel as a team?

1 We tend to become attached to our own ideas, and have a hard time letting go them, but when other people chip in, we can come up with even better versions.

2 Everyone's worldviews, experiences and areas of knowledge are different. Together, we can see the big picture.

3 Every person has a unique skill set. Some are good with numbers, others with words. But by pooling all their talents together, the sum is greater than the parts.

What can I do to make sure all of my teammates are happy?

Make decisions together, letting everyone contribute. Don't let one person dominate the conversation and talk over the others. Sometimes those who are the loudest and pushiest or those who are popular get heard the most, but try to listen to what every member has to say.

Notice the quiet ones; the ones sitting silently, away from the spotlight, observing. They probably have insights that will surprise everyone.

Appreciate the person who brings up difficult, but necessary questions. It's valuable to have someone on your team who is willing to discuss uncomfortable moments.

How can we come up with an idea together?

Have a brainstorming session! This is what one might look like:

PROJECT **ECO-TOWN**

Let everyone know the topic you will be discussing/problem you will be trying to solve ahead of time. For example, you need to come up with a public transport plan for your eco-town.

At the beginning of the session, go over the topic again and talk about the conditions your solution must have. For example, the public transport must be eco-friendly and not noisy.

Now it's actually time to brainstorm! All members can and must express their ideas freely for this to work. Write down all the possibilities on a piece of paper or on sticky notes. Important: don't judge or discuss their ideas quite yet.

Discuss what characteristics the ideal solution has.

Look over the ideas you all came up with and evaluate them against your ideal outcome. Vote on the best one.

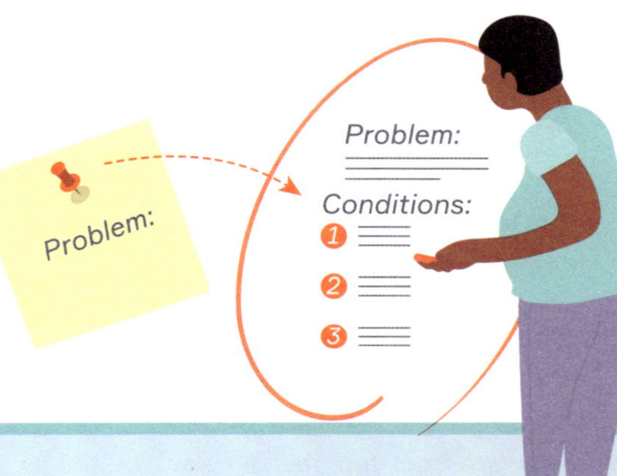

How should I hear everyone out?

If you're planning on having a discussion, **write down the things** you want to bring up beforehand. Let everyone add on to the list and choose someone to keep track of it and make sure that you get to each point.

Another person should **watch the time**. This person should warn the team when time has reached the halfway mark, when a quarter of the time remains, and when there's ten minutes left.

Interrupting cow whooo? Don't let it be you! If the discussion gets heated and everyone has a lot to say, use a talking piece. Pick an object, like a marker or a keychain, and pass it around. The person who is holding the object is the only one allowed to talk.

How do I understand my parents and help them understand me?

At times it might appear that your parents overly limit your freedom. Parents aren't always right, but they usually want what's best for you. If you talk to your parents openly and both parties are willing to be sincere, you'll be able to understand where they're coming from and vice versa.

They force me to go to bed early

Why? They've learned from their own mistakes how hard it is to get up early and get things done after staying up late. Getting a good night's sleep works wonders on your overall mood, your stability and ability to focus. Kids and teens need more sleep than adults do — around 8–10 hours of sleep per night. When running on fumes, you get irritable, frenzied and emotionally fragile.

What should I do? See for yourself! Compare how you feel when:

 You get a good night's rest

 You stay up until midnight texting friends, watching Netflix and doing homework

Draw conclusions and build your sleeping schedule around what makes you feel most energized and ready to face the day.

They want me to help out at home

Why? It feels good to live in a clean house, find your clothes clean and folded in your closet, and eat a warm breakfast every morning. Those things aren't done by house elves; they require a lot of work on your parents' part. When you get your own place, you can live however you want. But while you're sharing a home with your parents, you need to carry your weight.

They always criticize me

Why? Your parents aren't trying to show you that they're good and you're bad. They want to help you learn from your mistakes and be the best version of yourself. They can get carried away. It's possible that they don't even know how it hurts you to hear critcism after criticism.

What should I do? Think about what bothers you: their tone or what they're saying? Try to look past their way of expressing their thoughts (which might be getting an emotional reaction from you) and focus on the content. Is it a valid criticism? Tell your parents that you would appreciate it if they paused before repsonding and chose a different way of conveying their meaning to you. Or ask for positive feedback too, which will help you feel like you're doing something right.

What should I do? Make a list of chores that need to be done around the house and delegate them. Even if your input is minor, like cleaning up after yourself, it will lighten your parents' load.

They won't stay out of my business

Why? Your parents often see you as an extension of themselves. They want to protect you from pain and disappointment. They want you to be successful and happy.

What should I do? Talk to your parents and draw boundaries around what they can be involved in. For example, you're okay with them monitoring your grades, but they can't tell you what to wear or who your friends should be. If you want to be responsible for your own life, show them that you are capable of making good decisions.

They only care about my grades

Why? Your parents grew up with the formula "good grades = good college = successful life." Of course they want you to be financially stable and secure in the future. Grades don't show how smart you are, but they can signal how well you're keeping up.

What should I do? Tell your parents that you feel like they only love you for good grades. Let them know that you need support in other areas in your life, like showing an interest in your hobbies.

Dreaming of love

Most people dream of finding love. What a lot of them don't know is that finding it is the easy part. Building and maintaining a healthy, long-term relationship is the real challenge, but ultimately worth the effort.

Love or infatuation?

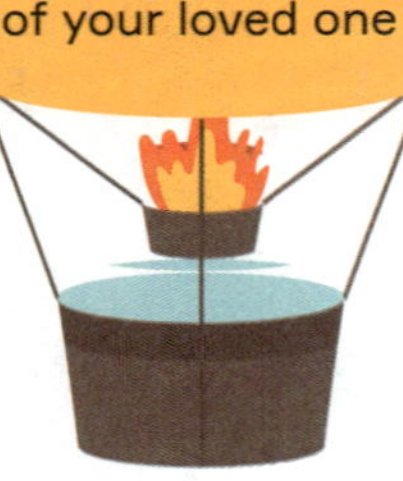

Love

- Born out of real emotional closeness, truly knowing who someone is as a person
- Includes the other person's imperfections; you love the good, the bad and the ugly
- Will grow stronger with time
- Can withstand arguments and challenges
- You take care of your loved one

Infatuation

- Can be felt towards a complete stranger
- You idolize the object of your affection and refuse to see their flaws
- Fleeting; it either disappears or turns into love
- Causes you to act irrationally
- You strive to be close to the object of your affection

The first step to love

The first step to love, however surprising it may be, is loving yourself. When you're able to validate yourself and feel whole on your own, you will be a better, more independent and more balanced partner. Not to mention that having self-respect will help you steer clear of toxic relationships and people.

Remember:

- *You're the only one responsible for your happiness*
- *You have the right to feel however you feel*
- *You can be different at different times; good, bad, strong, weak, etc.*
- *You're allowed to make mistakes*

How to build a romantic relationship:

Only get into a relationship if you are truly interested in the other person, not because of the societal pressure to be in one.

Learn as much as you can about the other person. This is why people go on dates, not because everyone else does it or just because someone asks you out.

Don't forget to have a life outside of your relationship. Make time for your hobbies and other important people in your life.

If something upsets or bothers you, talk about it with your partner. Keeping it to yourself won't make it go away.

What kind of relationships do you have?

Healthy relationships are built on a foundation of respect, equality, security and trust. Let's find out what shape the close relationships in your life are in. For every affirmative answer, give yourself a point. For every negative one, don't give yourself any.

Respect. You see your friend's phone light up with a text message. Will you read what it says while she isn't looking?

Equality. You're planning on hanging out with a buddy over the weekend. Are you the only one who gets a say in what you'll be doing?

Security. You've had a rough day and your friend happens to say something insensitive. Will you bite back?

Trust. The person you like shares something private with you. Are you going to tell your best friend about it?

If your total is zero, then your relationships are in tip-top shape. If it's greater than zero, think about what might be the problem and how you can fix it.

How can I love someone unconditionally?

Unconditional love is not just a cliche phrase, it has deep meaning. Loving people unconditionally means accepting them for who they really are deep down and helping them feel comfortable enough to express their real self.

Unconditional love looks like:

Allowing someone to be in charge of her own life and make her own decisions

Offering your help, advice and support

Asking rather than demanding

Not criticizing or judging, but trying to understand their motives and actions

How to leave a relationship

Unhealthy relationships

There's no mutual respect, security or trust

You're only happy when you're around your partner

One person tries to control the other

One cannot accept the other's self-sufficiency and independence

Support turns into self-sacrifice; you forget about your own interests and problems

Why is honesty important?

If you've lost interest or don't want to be in the relationship anymore for any reason, be honest about it with your partner. Hiding it only leads to more hurt: not just from the separation, but from the knowledge that you lied to your partner. Treat the other person the way you would like to be treated.

It's better to tell them face-to-face, rather than over text or on the phone. When you accept the responsibility for the difficult aspects of a relationship, you'll more confidently and maturely build relationships in the future.

It's unfair to:

Avoid meeting and hope your partner will get the message

Pretend like you're still interested

What's next?

Think about:

These questions will help you understand yourself better. Come back to them once every couple of months.

- Who are your friends? Who are your acquaintances?
- What do you and your close circle have in common? If you were friends with a different group of people, would your interests, values and goals be different?
- How do you act around your friends? Do you express yourself freely, make jokes, complain, stay silent?
- How would you like to act? What stands in the way of that?
- Do you and your parents understand each other? Can you have an open, honest conversation with them?
- What do you value in the people closest to you? What do they value in you?

What to read:

- **Be Brave. Be Your Best Self Every Day**
  by Editors of Teen Breathe

- **How to Win Friends and Influence People**
  by Dale Carnegie

What to watch:

What makes a good life?
by Robert Waldinger

5 ways to create stronger connections
by Robert Reffkin

CHAPTER 6

My body and I

- **Why should I care about my health?**

- **How does my diet affect me?**

- **How do my gadgets affect me?**

- **Why are cigarettes, alcohol and drugs bad for me?**

- **How does exercise affect me?**

- **What's next?**

Why should I care about my health?

Your body is your home where you should live in comfort and peace. And a home needs regular upkeep. Otherwise, pipes leak, appliances break and you're left with a lot of repair work to do... That is, if the problems are still fixable. The key difference between a body and a house is that you can't move out of your body and get a new one. So how can you keep things in order?

Being healthy means:

Living an abundant, colorful life, without having to worry about a lack of **strength or energy**

Having the opportunity **to try new things** without looking back on the limitations that your body sets

Attending to your body with love and care, like a **price-less gift**

Don't put it off! After the damage has been done, there's no guarantee that you'll be able to fix it. Don't wait until there's a serious issue to start taking care of yourself.

The younger you are, the easier it is to form new habits, including ones that help you look after your physical and mental health. If you make an effort to form these health habits now, taking care of yourself will only get easier with time.

Restoring your health is a long, expensive process. And the more you let it decay, the more money and time you'll end up spending to fix it.

Two hundred years ago the average human lifespan was around forty years. Today it's above seventy. With each new decade, we learn more about how to live a long and fruitful life. That's why "living a healthy lifestyle" has become a popular topic.

How can I tell if something's wrong?

If something is hurting, your body is sending you a signal. Don't dismiss it, especially if it keeps persisting, and if you don't know what's causing the pain, go see a doctor.

Pay attention to changes in your physical abilities and energy levels: for example, if you can usually run a mile without any problems, but today you found yourself winded and had to stop, there's a chance that something might be wrong.

Pay attention to outward physical changes, too: your skin, teeth, hair, nails, the color of your face. Internal issues will also show up externally.

How do I prolong my good health for many years?

Be conscious of what you put in your body: a balanced diet is the foundation of good health (for more, flip to p. 92).

Stay active! Exercise is just as important as what you eat. It's difficult to start exercising regularly after years of being a couch potato, so it's best to make it part of your routine early on (for more, flip to p. 98).

Don't forget to take care of yourself mentally and emotionally too! Your mental health can become a hazard to your physical health if it gets bad enough (to learn how to process feelings in a healthy way, flip to p. 52).

Don't I have my parents to worry about my health?

Your body is yours alone, which makes it your responsibility. Nobody can tell how you feel or what your body needs better than you can. It's your job to form habits that help maintain your health and practice them regularly, and do away with bad ones. Don't be afraid to ask your parents for help or advice, or to go see a doctor for a professional opinion.

How does my diet affect me?

We often say, "You are what you eat." What does this mean? Does our diet really affect us that much?

Does it make a difference when I eat?

1
Don't skip breakfast! It's the most important meal of the day, as it fuels you and gives you energy until nighttime.

2
Don't snack instead of eating a full meal!

3
Eat when you're hungry and don't eat when you're not. Your body knows what it needs and when.

Carbs are our most important source of energy for mental and physical activity. They affect our mood, memory and brain power more than the other food groups.

?

I don't like the taste of vegetables. Can I not eat them?

Fruits and vegetables contain many important vitamins crucial to our body, and different greens have different vitamins. They also contain fiber, which help clear our digestive system of digested food and make us feel full.

Protein is the building block of our muscles and other tissues. It also serves as the foundation for enzymes, which allow us to digest our food.

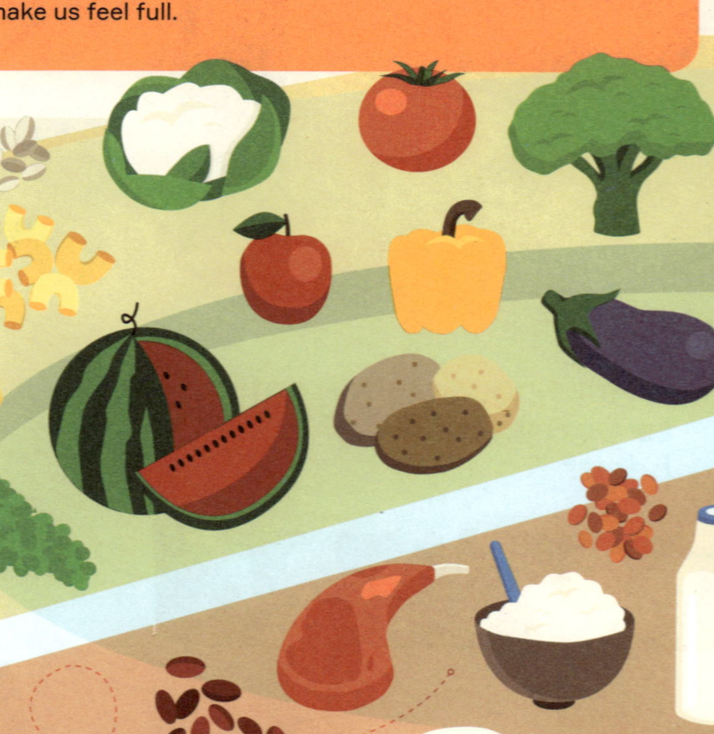

Why is it important to stay hydrated?

Your body is 60–70% water, so drinking water is even more important than eating. Even when slightly dehydrated, you might start feeling tired and irritable. The hotter and drier the climate is, the more water you should be drinking. It's important to note that feeling thirsty can often be confused with feeling hungry, so drink a glass of water before chomping down on a protein bar, then wait five minutes, and see if you're still craving something after.

Fats serve as our energy piggy bank. Our body can use fat tissue to store energy for a long time. Fats also help produce hormones, build cells (including brain cells) and keep us warm.

Not all fats are of equal value. Trans fats, which are found in processed foods, are very harmful to our bodies. So watch out for fast food and even plastic-wrapped beef jerky.

Could I survive on mac and cheese?

...Yes, but not for long. You see, for our bodies to function well and correctly, they need a diverse range of vitamins and minerals. Unfortunately, no one has invented a superfood that contains all that our bodies need yet. The responsibility falls to you; vary your diet as much as you can.

What should I eat: a chicken leg or chicken nuggets?

"Real" fresh food is always better than processed food. Pick a piece of steak over meatballs, chicken over chicken nuggets and potatoes over french fries. Generally, ready store-bought meals contain a lot of added preservatives and other chemicals, which can easily bring about addiction, so use caution.

Can a piece of chocolate save me?

When you're exhausted, you may find yourself reaching for the candy jar. Sugar may give you quick and easy energy, but its effects are fleeting, and afterwards you will feel even more tired. And with each subsequent fix, you'll have to take an even bigger piece to restore your strength.

1. Be extra careful about what you buy: there's sugar in practically everything now, even bread and sausage, nevermind the copious amounts in juice, muffins, cookies and bread.

2. When craving something sweet, it's better to eat a piece of candy than to drink a glass of juice. You know how much sugar the candy has, but can't be sure about the juice!

3. An even better cure for an aching sweet tooth — eat some fruit.

How do my gadgets affect me?

Ever been scared to look at your **screen time data**? The average person spends two hours on the phone every day. We sacrifice real connection, our health and personal development... and for what?

Here's what you train your brain to do by being absorbed in your phone:

Get distracted every four seconds. How often do you find yourself reaching for your phone in the middle of doing homework or during social time, to scroll through your feed, read your messages, look through photos? You train your "monkey mind" to jump from one task to the other. The more you give in to the impulse, the harder it becomes to remain focused and complete tasks in one sitting.

Rely on instant gratification. When you watch a funny tiktok or check the amount of likes on a post, your brain releases dopamine, or the pleasure hormone, almost as if you were eating sugar. This reaction is triggered on purpose by companies that want to keep us hooked on their products as much as fast food chains do.

Struggle with interpreting complex reactions. Reaction gifs, likes and comments aren't good representations for the genuine emotions we experience. Interpreting responses in real life gets progressively harder: you can't understand what people are trying to convey, why they're reacting the way they are, what's written on their face... and your own responses and reactions will become harder to regulate.

Replace real relationships with the illusion of connection. Messaging or commenting online may feel like socializing, but it doesn't even come close to the real thing. The majority of your "followers" don't actually know you or care about you.

Pre-occupied with gadgets only. Watching Netflix and YouTube becomes our main leisure activities and we forget to have hobbies. Then when we decide to do something else, our brain, which is already used to things that are designed to keep our attention at all cost, gets bored and wants its entertainment back. So the cycle continues.

Lose imagination. Your phone and computer strip you of your ability to invent, problem-solve and create. These traits are valuable because they're exactly what sets us apart from artificial intelligence.

Time people spend on their phone

~ 2 hours every day

People checks their phone

~ 85 times a day

How do I stop "getting stuck" in my phone?

1

Keep track of how many hours you spend on your phone, computer and TV. For a week, write down every time you reach for a gadget and record every minute you spend on it. What's your total?

2

Clean your digital space of everything that doesn't spark joy and is cluttering up your storage. Figure out which apps you use and for what. Make three groups: *important* (to keep), *not sure* (take some time to observe yourself and figure out if they're valuable) and *delete* (definitely not important). Be clear on how the functions of the apps you keep add to your life.

4

Decide what you actually want to do in your free time. Maybe you've always wanted to learn how to play the guitar? It's time to find something just as interesting to fill that newly-available time.

3

Commit to not using the "not sure" apps from method number two for a month and see how that impacts your life. Then, at the end of the month, make a choice whether you really need them (probably not).

5

There's no need to completely cut out social media, video games and TV shows from your life. But **setting aside a limited amount of time for these activities** in advance won't only help you regulate them, but it will also make them more enjoyable. Put this free time in your schedule and then you can shamelessly indulge in your favorite Netflix show, while updating your social media.

6

Choose real-life interactions over digital ones as often as you can. Call instead of texting, and meet in person instead of calling. Real interaction is always the best option.

Can I just stop doing homework for a second to check whether anyone's texted me?

It may seem like checking your phone will only take a moment but, in reality, your flow will have been disrupted and you'll need more than a minute to gather yourself again, find your spot and restore your train of thought before you start working again.

Why are cigarettes, alcohol and drugs bad for me?

"Just try it! One time won't hurt you!" These are the words of someone who's just looking for a new "experience". You might be inclined to believe this person, but if you could see what the consequences of lighting up a cigarette or downing a beer are, you'd think twice and turn down the invitation.

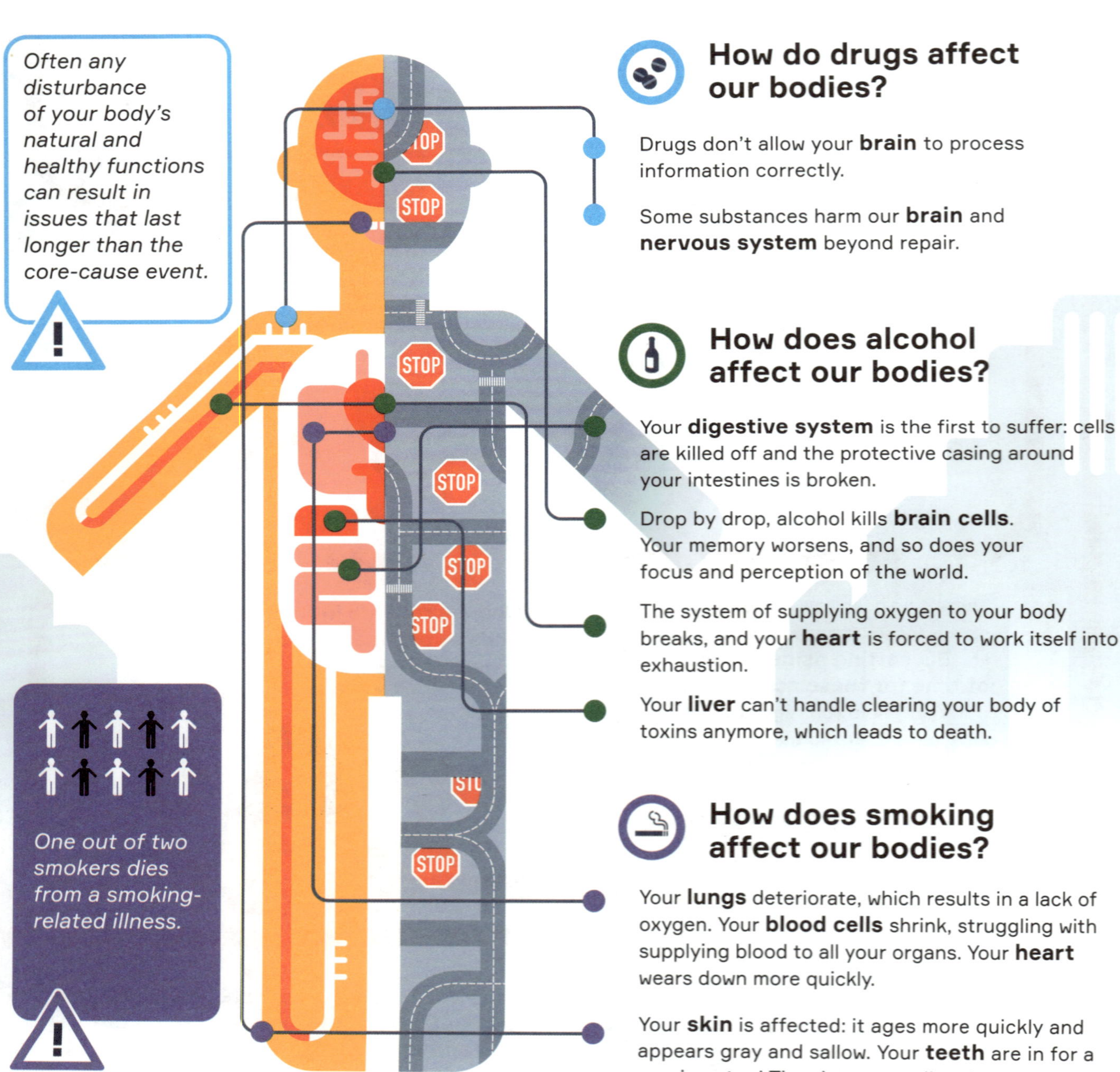

How do drugs affect our bodies?

Drugs don't allow your **brain** to process information correctly.

Some substances harm our **brain** and **nervous system** beyond repair.

How does alcohol affect our bodies?

Your **digestive system** is the first to suffer: cells are killed off and the protective casing around your intestines is broken.

Drop by drop, alcohol kills **brain cells**. Your memory worsens, and so does your focus and perception of the world.

The system of supplying oxygen to your body breaks, and your **heart** is forced to work itself into exhaustion.

Your **liver** can't handle clearing your body of toxins anymore, which leads to death.

How does smoking affect our bodies?

Your **lungs** deteriorate, which results in a lack of oxygen. Your **blood cells** shrink, struggling with supplying blood to all your organs. Your **heart** wears down more quickly.

Your **skin** is affected: it ages more quickly and appears gray and sallow. Your **teeth** are in for a surpirse, too! They become yellow, just like your lips. And, as a bonus, you'll always smell bad.

If all these habits are so harmful, then why don't people quit them?

Our brains love pleasure. When we smoke, take drugs or drink alcohol, our body releases chemicals that give us a temporary high. Our brain remembers this shortcut to happiness (like a dog that will fetch a stick for treats) and will want to use it again and again.

The problem is each time we have to up the dosage for it to have the same effect. Even then, the pleasure itself doesn't last as long and becomes less and less intense.

Your body stops producing the natural chemicals designed to make you feel happy, and things that you used to enjoy and wish for don't bring you happiness anymore.

It's really hard to quit: you struggle physically and mentally. You don't feel happy or see the point in living anymore, and the world around you seems bleak and meaningless.

> **Just remember: when you start using artificial sources of happiness, such as chemicals, you give up the real experience of happiness and harm your health. And it's a choice that's entirely up to you.**

Is it true that standing next to a smoker is just as detrimental as smoking yourself?

Yes, second-hand smoke is harmful. Around one in eight people who die of smoke-related illness haven't smoked a day in their lives.

What should I do if my friends smoke? I'm not just gonna stop hanging out with them.

Ask them to not smoke when they're around you. Your loved ones will understand and respect your wishes. And remember: we are heavily affected by the people we choose to surround ourselves with.

How does exercise affect me?

Take kids as an example: they're constantly on their feet, running, playing and moving. As we get older, we slow down and it becomes routine to spend our days crouching over textbooks or at our computers. But, even though we might not notice, our bodies feel the detrimental effects of a lack of exercise.

Do I not exercise enough?

Perform an experiment: count how much time you spend sitting down every day. You might be surprised, but it's likely over 8 hours! (This is around the same amount of time you spend lying down in your bed when you sleep). You sit down to eat, to do your homework, to watch TV, to relax so, as a result, your body doesn't use up a lot of energy, your muscles get weaker, your resilience lowers, you gain extra fat and your spine and joints deteriorate.

What if I don't have time to exercise?

Working out and getting your body moving aren't the same thing. Of course, signing up for kickboxing or getting a gym membership is great: these things teach you discipline and develop your willpower. But if you're only able to do them twice a week, and live a sedentary lifestyle otherwise, then they can be harmful; the sudden strain to your body can actually cause injury. Start with small goals — just get moving! Stretch, go for long walks with your dog, stop using the elevator, try doing your homework standing up (for example, when you don't have to write, but are trying to memorize something).

How much should I exercise?

At least 30 minutes a day! But the more, the better. Take baby steps towards an active lifestyle; slowly increase the amount and intensity over time. And remember that recovery is important. Or, in other words, health comes from an even balance of work and rest.

> *Even though we've been conditioned otherwise through evolution, most people nowadays lead a passive lifestyle. Over the course of human history, we have had to look for food, hunt, work in the fields and take care of livestock. Thus, our bodies were built for movement.*

Why do we need movement?

It improves brain function
When your body is moving, your brain more actively releases chemicals that help you think faster and understand information better. Go on a 15–20-minute walk or run — it's gonna be much easier to get your homework done afterwards.

It helps us deal with stress
Exercise causes endorphins to be released into our bodies, which lowers our stress levels. If you're feeling tense, try going for a run — no doubt you'll feel a lot better.

Downtime
Want to put your brain on pause? Any physical activity will allow you to do just that. When you're worn out and can't concentrate, run, walk or even dance to your favorite song.

It develops willpower
Exercising daily is one of the most beneficial habits that you can cultivate.

It slows down the process of aging
Regular exercise prevents your muscles from aging, strengthens the general makeup of your body and stimulates your metabolism. You won't have to worry about that for a while, since you're still growing up. But, if you adjust to that type of activity now, your older self will thank you!

It enhances your appearance
You don't necessarily have to live at the gym until you get a six-pack. Manageable but regular exercise will tone your muscles and make your body lean — you'll look great, but, more importantly, you will feel more confident.

It helps your mood
Even some light stretching to the sound of some uplifting music after you wake up will give you energy and start the day off on the right note.

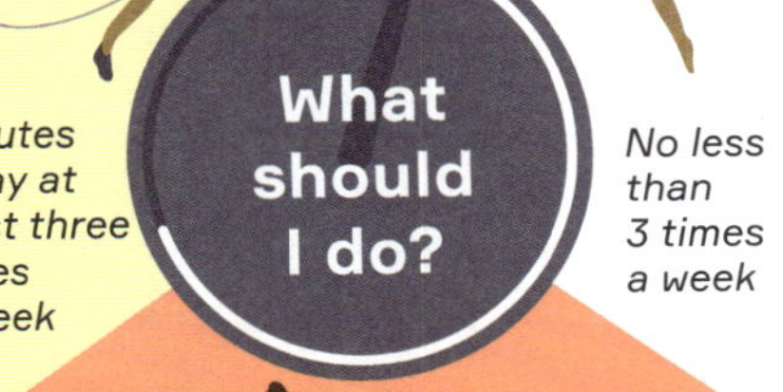

Aerobic exercises are a type of exercise during which the flow of oxygen into our bodies is increased (walking, running, biking, swimming and others).

Strength training includes exercises during which your muscle strength faces resistance or force (weights, pushups, TRX).

Flexibility training includes stretching, pilates and yoga.

What's next?

Think about:

These questions will help you understand yourself better. Come back to them once every couple of months.

- How much time have you spent sitting in one place today?
- How do you usually feel after working out or any type of active movement?
- How do you feel when you get eight hours of sleep? What about when you get less than six?
- Keep a tally for one day and see how many times a day you check your phone. How often did you look at your texts or social media?
- Try to go a month without eating sugar and junk food. Eat less meat and replace it with fruits and vegetables. Take a "before" and "after" photo: how is your body, skin and hair different?

What to read:

- **How the Body Works: The Facts Simply Explained** by Virginia Smith, Nicola Temple and Mark Clifton

- **No Weigh! A Teen's Guide to Positive Body Image, Food, and Emotional Wisdom** by Shelley Aggarwal, Signe Darpinian and Wendy Sterling

Your tools:

- Habit tracker
- Apps that track your phone usage
- Reusable waterbottle

What to watch:

**Sleep is your
superpower**
by Matt Walker

**How the food you eat
affects your brain**
by Mia Nacamulli

References

1. Aggarwal S., Darpinian S., Sterling W. *No Weigh! A Teen's Guide to Positive Body Image, Food, and Emotional Wisdom.* Jessica Kingsley Publishers, 2018

2. Alex Soojung-Kim Pang. *The Distraction Addiction: Getting the Information You Need and the Communication You Want, Without Enraging Your Family, Annoying Your Colleagues, and Destroying Your Soul.* Little, Brown and Company, 2013

3. Allen D., Williams M., Wallace M. *Getting Things Done for Teens: Take Control of Your Life in a Distracting World.* Penguin Books, 2018

4. The Arbinger Institute. *The Anatomy of Peace: Resolving the Heart of Conflict.* Berrett-Koehler Publishers, 2015

5. Armstrong T. *You're Smarter Than You Think: A Kid's Guide to Multiple Intelligences.* Free Spirit Publishing, 2002

6. Bachel Beverly K. *What Do You Really Want? How to Set a Goal and Go for It!* Free Spirit Publishing, 2016

7. Baumeister R., Tierney J. *Willpower: Rediscovering the Greatest Human Strength.* Penguin Books, 2012

8. Ben-Shahar T. *Happier. Learn the Secrets to Daily Joy and Lasting Fulfillment.* McGraw-Hill Education, 2007

9. Berne E. *Games People Play.* Ballantine Books, 1996

10. Boaler J. *Limitless Mind: Learn, Lead, and Live Without Barriers.* HarperOne, 2019

11. Bono E. *Six Thinking Hats.* Back Bay Books, 1999

12. Bourbeau L. *Amour, Amour, Amour: La Puissance de l'acceptation.* BookBaby, 2016

13. Bradberry T., Greaves J. *Emotional Intelligence 2.0.* TalentSmart, 2009

14. Camp J. *Start with No: The Negotiating Tools That the Pros Don't Want You to Know.* Currency, 2002

15. Canfield J., Hansen M., Hewitt L. *The Power of Focus: How to Hit Your Business, Personal and Financial Targets with Absolute Confidence and Certainty.* Health Communications Incorporated, 2012

16. Carnegie D. *How to Win Friends and Influence People.* Vermilion, 2012

17. Chade-Meng Tan, Goleman D., Kabat-Zinn J. *Search Inside Yourself: The Unexpected Path to Achieving Success, Happiness (and World Peace).* HarperOne, 2014

18. Christakis N., Fowler J. *Connected. The Surprising Power of Our Social Networks and How They Shape Our Lives.* Little, Brown Spark, 2011

19. Christensen C., Allworth J., Dillon K. *How Will You Measure Your Life?* Harper Business, 2012

20. Cialdini R. *Influence: The Psychology of Persuasion.* Harper Business, 2006

21. Cialdini R., Goldstein N., Martin S. *Yes!: 50 Scientifically Proven Ways to Be Persuasive.* Penguin Publishing Group, 2018

22. Clear J. *Atomic Habits: An Easy & Proven Way to Build Good Habits & Break Bad Ones.* Penguin Publishing Group, 2018

23. Covey S. *The 7 Habits of Highly Effective Teens.* Simon & Schuster, 2014

24. Covey S. R. *The 7 Habits of Highly Effective People.* Free Press, 1989

25. Duckworth A. *Grit: The Power of Passion and Perseverance.* Scribner Book Company, 2016

26. Duhigg Ch. *The Power of Habit: Why We Do What We Do in Life and Business.* Random House Trade Paperbacks, 2014

27. Dweck C. S. *Mindset. The New Psychology of Success. How We Can Learn to Fulfill Our Potential.* Ballantine Books, 2007

28. Edge Ch., Mulholland P. *How to be a Young #Writer.* OUP Oxford, 2017

29. Faber A., Mazlish E. *How to Talk So Kids Will Listen & Listen So Kids Will Talk.* Scribner Book Company, 2012

30. Ferrari B. T. *Power Listening: Mastering the Most Critical Business Skill of All.* Portfolio, 2012

31. Fisher R., Ury W., Patton B. *Getting to Yes: Negotiating Agreement Without Giving In.* Penguin Books, 2011

32. Fleming K. *The Leader's Guide to Emotional Agility: How to Use Soft Skills to Get Hard Results.* FT Press, 2015

33. Foer J. S. *We Are the Weather: Saving the Planet Begins at Breakfast.* Farrar, Straus and Giroux, 2019

34. Forster M. *Do It Tomorrow and Other Secrets of Time Management.* Hodder & Stoughton, 2008

35. Geel J. *Pitching Ideas: Make People Fall in Love with Your Ideas.* Laurence King Publishing, 2018

36. Gerzon M. *Leading Through Conflict. How Successful Leaders Transform Differences into Opportunities.* Harvard Business Review Press, 2006

37. Gladwell M. *Talking to Strangers: What We Should Know about the People We Don't Know.* Little, Brown and Company, 2019

38. Goins J. *The Art of Work: A Proven Path to Discovering What You Were Meant to Do.* HarperCollins Leadership, 2015

39. Goldsmith M., Reiter M. *Triggers: Creating Behavior That Lasts — Becoming the Person You Want to Be.* Currency, 2015

40. Goleman D. *Emotional Intelligence: Why It Can Matter More Than IQ.* Random House Publishing Group, 2005

41. Greger M. *How Not to Die. Discover the Foods Scientifically Proven to Prevent and Reverse Disease.* Flatiron Books, 2015

42. Guise S. *Mini Habits: Smaller Habits, Bigger Results.* Createspace Independent Publishing Platform, 2014

43. Harris S. *Lying.* Four Elephants Press, 2013

44. Hatcher J. P., McDonagh T. *101 Ways to Conquer Teen Anxiety: Simple Tips, Techniques and Strategies for Overcoming Anxiety, Worry and Panic Attacks.* Ulysses Press, 2016

45. Hawkins D. R. *Letting Go: The Pathway of Surrender.* Hay House Inc., 2014

46. Heath Ch., Heath D. *Made to Stick: Why Some Ideas Survive and Others Die.* Random House, 2007

47. Holiday R. *The Obstacle Is the Way: The Timeless Art of Turning Trials into Triumph.* Portfolio, 2014

48. Hurley D. *Smarter. The New Science of Building Brain Power.* Plume, 2014

49. Jeffers S. *Feel the Fear and Do It Anyway: Dynamic Techniques for Turning Fear, Indecision and Anger into Power, Action and Love.* Jeffers Press, 2007

50. Kabat-Zinn J. *Full Catastrophe Living: Using the Wisdom of Your Body and Mind to Face Stress, Pain, and Illness.* Bantam, 2013

51. Keller G., Papasan J. *The ONE Thing: The Surprisingly Simple Truth Behind Extraordinary Results.* Bard Press, 2013

52. Kennedy G. *Everything is Negotiable! How to Get the Best Deal Every Time.* Random House Business, 2008

53. Kiyosaki R. T. *Rich Dad Poor Dad for Teens: The Secrets about Money — That You Don't Learn in School!* Plata Publishing, 2015

54. Koch R. *The 80/20 Principle: The Secret of Achieving More with Less.* Currency, 1999

55. Lau J. Y. F. *An Introduction to Critical Thinking and Creativity: Think More, Think Better.* Wiley, 2011

56. McAllister B., Marriner M., Gebhard N. *Roadmap: The Get-It-Together Guide for Figuring Out What to Do with Your Life.* Chronicle Books, 2015

57. McGonigal K. *The Willpower Instinct. How Self-Control Works, Why It Matters, and What You Can Do to Get More of It.* Avery, 2013

58. Moss M. *Salt, Sugar, Fat: How the Food Giants Hooked Us.* Random House Trade Paperbacks, 2014

59. Palladino L. J. *Find Your Focus Zone. An Effective New Plan to Defeat Distraction and Overload.* Atria Books, 2011

60. Rath T. *Eat, Move, Sleep: How Small Choices Lead to Big Changes.* Missionday, 2013

61. Robinson K., Aronica L. *The Element: How Finding Your Passion Changes Everything.* Penguin Books, 2009

62. Rosling H., Rosling Rönnlund A., Rosling O. *Factfulness: Ten Reasons We're Wrong About the World — and Why Things Are Better Than You Think.* Flatiron Books, 2018

63. Schewe O. *Super Student.* Jaico Publishing House, 2018

64. Sher B., Gottlieb A. *Wishcraft: How to Get What You Really Want.* Ballantine Books, 2004

65. Sincero J. *You Are a Badass: How to Stop Doubting Your Greatness and Start Living an Awesome Life.* Running Press, 2013

66. Singer M. *The Untethered Soul. The Journey Beyond Yourself.* New Harbinger Publications, 2007

67. Smith V., Temple N., Clifton M. *How the Body Works: The Facts Simply Explained.* DK Publishing, 2016

68. Stone D., Heen S. *Thanks for the Feedback: The Science and Art of Receiving Feedback Well.* Viking, 2014

69. Teen Breathe. *Be Brave. Be Your Best Self Every Day.* Ammonite Press, 2019

70. Tetlock P. E., Gardner D. *Superforecasting: The Art and Science of Prediction.* Crown Publishing, 2016

Notes

Life Skills 101: 80 Exercises to Master Them

Okay, so you've read the book. Now what? We've created 80 exercises to put theory into practice. Using this workbook along with *Life Skills 101: Everything You Need, But Won't Learn in School* serves as a double punch in the gut of your struggles, bad habits, and insecurities.

You'll have fun while growing into the person you want to become one exercise at a time.

Science-based non-fiction
For children around middle-school age

Life Skills 101: Everything You Need, But Won't Learn In School
A Visual Guide

Creator of original concept and editor-in-chief *Maria Gorina*
Responsible for publishing *Anastasia Trojan*
DTP design by *Elizabeth Kopai-Gora*
Layout by *Elizabeth Kopai-Gora, Ekaterina Aleksashkina*
Cover by *Anna Kirsanova*
Language editors *Laird Cenotto, Todd Jackson, Daria Baltrushaitis, Yulia Molokova, Natalia Erokhina*
Pre-press *Nadezda Kudryakova, Ekaterina Aleksashkina*
Translated by *Sofiya Ivanova*

Illustrated by Yulia Adelova, Lydia-Maria Veles, Yulia Volodina, Olga Dolgih, Anna Kirsanova, Elizabeth Kopai-Gora, Tatiana Makarova, Anastasia Ogurtsova, Elena Okoltsina, Yulia Osintseva, Alina Sibiryakova

For more information contact:
ivigreen.com
hello@ivigreen.com

ISBN 978-1-7378751-0-9